Date: 6/13/11

THE WISDOM
OF THE RADISH

And Other Lessons Learned on a Small Farm

Lynda Hopkins

SASQUATCH BOOKS
SEATTLE

Printed in the United States of America
Published by Sasquatch Books
Distributed by PGW/Perseus
17 16 15 14 13 12 11   9 8 7 6 5 4 3 2 1

Cover photograph: Lilia Ahner
Cover design: Jessika Merrill
Interior design and composition: Sarah Plein
Interior photographs: Lynda Hopkins

Library of Congress Cataloging-in-Publication Data
Hopkins, Lynda.
The wisdom of the radish and other lessons learned on a small farm / Lynda Hopkins.
    p. cm.
Includes bibliographical references.
ISBN-13: 978-1-57061-642-6
ISBN-10: 1-57061-642-6
1. Farm life—California—Healdsburg. 2. Country life—California—Healdsburg. I. Title.
S521.5.C2H67 2011
630.9794—dc22

                        2010047955

Sasquatch Books
119 South Main Street, Suite 400
Seattle, WA 98104
(206) 467-4300
www.sasquatchbooks.com
custserv@sasquatchbooks.com

To Emmett, my fellow farmer

. . . .

CONTENTS

· ·

The Beginning:

SEED

. . . .

**It's 4:30 a.m. on a Saturday: the start of my workweek, if a
week without an end can be said to have a start.**

As usual, I'm awake—having opened my eyes ten minutes
before the alarm's shrill beeps—but wakefulness does not cor-
respond to readiness. At the moment, I'm firmly fixed in a
state of denial. It isn't 4:30 in the morning, I'm not going to
work, I didn't spend another Friday night harvesting instead
of drinking, I'm not about to sprint around a field brandishing
scissors and a buck knife in the predawn gloom.

It will be approximately half an hour before I admit that
yes it is, yes I am, yes I did, yes I will—and I'll actually enjoy it,
despite the epithets that slip out of my mouth every few minutes.

Last night, we harvested the less perishable items: golden
and green zucchinis, Armenian cucumbers, Chioggia and golden
beets, French Breakfast and Champion radishes, and baby bok
choy (which is definitely perishable, but slightly less so than our
other greens). We hand-watered the beet, broccoli, and carrot
seedlings with our trusty galvanized steel watering can, knowing
that the following morning we'd be too rushed and groggy to
remember to do it—and that if we didn't moisten their topsoil,
the tender little guys might not survive our day's absence.

At 9:00 p.m., we finished watering and tucked floating row covers over the seedlings, readying them for bed. The sky gathered darkness in the east. To the west, gold-flecked cirrus clouds accented the silhouette of a pine-serrated ridge. In the evening wind, the field danced: the beans, which have outgrown their ten-foot-tall fencing, waved long, skinny tendrils in the breeze. The row covers fluttered, white ripples across the ground. The corn plants rattled, and the tomatoes strained against their supporting twine, stems full of bobbing green fruit. Stealing a brief moment to take it all in, I turned in a slow circle before joining Emmett in the Gator. He flicked on the headlights and put the pedal to the metal: we raced away from the field at a good ten miles per hour, filling the night with our dust.

But the day wasn't quite over. Back at home, I stayed up to satisfy my personal addiction: posting to my farm blog. In bed, I lay awake for an hour thinking about how little sleep I was about to get. The longer I thought about it, the less sleep I got, and the more I thought about it.

Which brings me to 4:40 a.m. My work pants and shirt are on, as is the light. I'm shoveling Cheerios into my face, gulping down lemonade—no time to brew tea and we're out of juice—and slowly transitioning from simply awake to ready to go.

In the car, Emmett drives, I pull on socks and shoes, and we're on the field before the clock ticks over to five. The coolers—all six of them—come out of the car and onto the dirt. I unfold the card table that we use for sorting salad and put a clean pink bath towel on it.

Time to cut.

We have salad down to a science. We each grab a pair of scissors. Emmett heads for the brassicas (a mix of baby kale, tatsoi, mizuna, arugula, and mustard greens) and I head for the lettuces (a mix of baby Blackhawk, Firecracker, red

Salad Bowl, Tango, Parris Island, Deer Tongue, and Rouge d'Hiver—or, in layman's terms: red, green, flat, and curly).

The metallic sound of scissoring slices through the frigid morning air. My hands, up to the wrists in dewy lettuce, quickly lose feeling. The light is blue and the birds haven't yet started chirping. As I snip fistfuls of lettuce and toss them into the harvest bin, I keep a watchful eye out for weeds, mushrooms, slugs, cucumber beetles, and bug-savaged leaves. Things always slip through; although we'll give the lettuce a second once-over as we scoop it from the bin into plastic bags, our quality control still leaves something to be desired. We've been meaning to build a long screen table for more effective sorting, but who has the time? On this weekend alone, we'll each put in twenty-six hours of work on the farm—and that's not counting Friday night.

So, for now, we still find cucumber beetles and weeds sneaking out of our salad bags at the farmers' market, sometimes in front of customers. On the bright side, I'm pretty sure none of the weeds are toxic.

We each fill two tubs with our respective salad mixes. Emmett runs a hose into the brassica bins to rid them of cucumber and flea beetles. We'll let the bugs float to the top while we harvest the Lacinato kale, then spread the brassicas on the pink towel to air-dry. The lettuces don't attract nearly as many insects, so they go straight into the bags without washing.

En route to the kale, I walk by the hip-high potato plants, which recently burst into bloom—purple flowers for the purple potatoes, white for the russets—and think back two months ago to when we first planted the potatoes.

That, actually, is where this tale should begin. A farm does not start at five o'clock on an efficient market morning. It starts out with mistakes and uncertainty. Two months ago, Emmett and I couldn't figure out which way was up. Literally.

We were arguing over whether the things coming out of the potato were sprouts or roots. The things were several inches long, knobby, with a few elbows apiece. Pure white, too: not even the barest tinge of green. Six of them sprouted in a cluster, breaking through wrinkled brown skin.

"Emmett," I called out across the field. "I have a question."

He bounded over to where I knelt, clasping a sprouted russet potato, in the dust. "This thing," I said, "Is it a sprout or a root? Which way is up?"

"I think it's a sprout. So I think *that* way's up," he said, turning the potato around in my hand so that the things pointed skyward.

"Damn, I thought it was a root. Look, see how there are lots of them? Don't plants usually send up just one stem? And this potato has been exposed to light. Wouldn't the stem be producing chlorophyll by now? And why aren't there leaves, anyway?"

Emmett was unable to defend his hypothesis with anything more than a shrug, so we decided to postpone potato planting until the time when we could conclusively determine which way was up.

Being twenty-first-century farmers, we often turn to the Internet as our number-one resource. But the Internet, for all its information on potato blight, potato pests, potato wine, potato nicknames, and potato history, refused to yield any potatoes-for-idiots diagrams. After a half hour of fruitless searching, I still didn't know which end was up.

Clearly, we were in need of a guide. Heck, if we couldn't even figure out how to plant a *potato*, we were going to need a sage, amenable third-person companion to shepherd us through the entirety of the farm-starting process.

Having already failed with Google, I headed over to Amazon.

The search results sounded promising: *The Young Farmer's Manual, Vol. II: How to Make Farming Pay*; *The Elements of Agriculture: A Book for Young Farmers*; *The Young Farmer: Some Things He Should Know*.

Promising, that is, until I glanced at the original publication dates: 1867, 1868, and 1859 respectively. For the last 150 years, it would seem that young people haven't identified themselves as farmers in sufficient number to merit substantial publishing on the topic. Sure, the '60s and '70s yielded a rash of hand-illustrated primers on self-sustenance, aimed at a fresh crop of hippie back-to-the-landers. But these books were more about lifestyle and less about earning a living. Let's face it: the last time farming was seen as a viable, venerable career for young people—the sort of thing for which a two-volume manual might be written—women wore crinoline hoop skirts and were still decades away from the ballot box. (In that day and age, the use of the universal masculine pronoun in a title was presumably less likely to offend.)

Back then, farming was a respected way of life. Now it has practically fallen off the census as an occupation: less than 1 percent of Americans identify themselves as farmers.[1] Faced with colossal agribusinesses (Cargill, Tyson), farm-gobbling suburban sprawl (Anytown, USA), and cheap imports from overseas ($63 billion worth in 2009[2]), most farmers' kids don't have to think twice about which professional path *not* to take. In fact, the percentage of American farmers over the age of fifty-five has risen from 37 percent in 1954 to 61 percent in 1997.[3]

But the times, they are a-changing. And things are looking a little brighter for tomorrow's young farmers. The proliferation of farmers' markets—6,132 in the United States in August 2010[4]—farm stands, and locavore-friendly restaurants has opened up new doors for direct marketing opportunities, in effect creating a new local food economy. Small-scale farmers, rather than routing goods through multiple middlemen, now receive top dollar for their produce by selling it directly to their customers.

There are other signs of a sea change. The economy's down, but seed sales are up. Backyard chicken coops are spreading across the country like new strains of West Nile virus. Even Walmart is starting to source "locally" (that is, same-state). Small farms spring up where you'd least expect them—in abandoned city lots, on conservation easement properties, or sandwiched between blocs of Chardonnay and Pinot Noir vines in the heart of California's wine country.

So although young farmers may not have been the publishing world's hottest topic of the twentieth century, there's every reason to believe that they will feature prominently in the twenty-first. Where there's a business opportunity, there will be young people willing to take a risk—and taking a risk we are, in sufficient numbers to merit the naming of a movement.

Today's Greenhorn Movement is a growing force. Think of it as a cyber-savvy, more marketable version of the '60s back-to-the-land shebang, with equal parts idealism and business sense. Whatever way you look at it—skeptically as a passing phase, or hopefully as a permanent change in food production—the Greenhorn Movement is a catchy phenomenon. Recent articles in the *New York Times* and the *Los Angeles Times* have featured the new wave of young farmers. We're even the topic of a documentary film. But of course, the Web is where we really shine, discussing the trials and tribulations of our nascent farms on innumerable blogs, message boards, and other portals.

We can't take all the credit. The Greenhorn Movement stands on the shoulders of giants: intrepid authors and farmers who worked hard to draw a clear line between local, sustainable agriculture and resource-intensive factory farms. We owe thanks to farmers, ranchers, and landowners who stayed put rather than selling out to developers; and to the millions of Americans who are voting with their forks, frequenting farmers' markets to provide direct market opportunities for growers.

One of our strongest assets is one for which we're hardly responsible: our collective age. With the average age of Californian farmers at 58.4,[5] the addition of youth is crucial to the local food movement's longevity. Even as I thank customers for buying my produce at the farmers' market, I find myself being thanked in return—even worried over—by my customers. "How's it going for you?" one of my regulars likes to ask. "I mean, are you making it?" She means financially, and often, my answer has been noncommittal. "Well, I hope you do, because we need young farmers like you," she replies, charitably handing me three dollars for a bag of holey mixed greens. It's a refrain I hear time and time again, and it never gets old.

Which brings me back to my own little corner of the movement and why I'm here in the first place. My problem is that I love a farmer.

Well, a sort-of farmer.

Like many Greenhorns, I'm not a farmer's daughter, not a farmer's wife—in fact, I'm pretty sure I'm not even a farmer's first cousin, second cousin, niece, granddaughter, goddaughter, or aunt. To identify my class, I prefer to spin off from the more common concept of "farmer's wife." Just call me the "aspiring farmer's girlfriend." The awkward tentativeness of the phrase reflects the awkwardness of the movement. On our best days, we're toting tubs full of gorgeous, ripe organic produce to a hungry market. But on many days, we're not nearly as triumphant, trying to lay the groundwork for new sustainable agriculture systems in places they haven't been tried before. (And on *my* worst days, I'm downright confused, arguing over whether the long, skinny things coming out of the flaccid potato are roots or sprouts. As it turns out, Emmett had the better sense of direction.)

Emmett—the sort-of farmer I love—and I are both twenty-five, with a healthy appreciation for the environment. We enjoy cooking and eating food. Emmett even likes growing things, and has had success doing so in the past. So far, so good. But while he tended beets and radishes on the windowsill of his dorm room, I was busy pulling volunteer strawberries out of my mom's backyard, thinking them weeds.

Like a lot of young people, we had every intention of saving the world after graduating from college. But the more we thought about it, the less appealing it seemed to save the world from within the walls of a cubicle. I've always kept a mental tally of hands-on, worthwhile opportunities that can also potentially provide a living wage. For years, Emmett and I have sketched out innovative sustainable business plans, from a bicycle bagel-delivery service to an heirloom-garden planting business that would turn your lawn into an organic paradise.

Looking back, it seems inevitable that sooner or later we'd consider starting a sustainable farming business of our own. Theoretically, farming fulfills many of our shared lifestyle desires: to make the world a bit better, to become integral members of a local community, to spend time outside, to help people. We envisioned a farm that would provide the community with food healthful for both humans and environment, a farm that would also serve as an educational tool, a place for community members to visit and learn about sustainable agriculture. For people who couldn't afford the local, organic premium, we'd offer a work-trade program—a program in which participants work a few hours alongside farmers in exchange for a week's worth of free, fresh produce.

A farmer's job description holds considerable appeal to both of us. Emmett appreciated the idea of flexible work hours, since he'd previously been a nine-to-fiver. I appreciated the opportunity to write—even if just a farm blog or newsletter—and the potential to have more pets in my life (think: chickens) than I could in our previous tiny rentals. As a vegan who never stopped craving eggs and cheese, I could try to find ethical alternatives to confined large-scale production. And of course, add to these desires the simple joy of growing: the improbability of a tiny seed turning into a sprawling squash plant, the gloriously dirty fingernails, the satisfaction of an honest day's work.

Just as important, we needed an income, and a small farm business now has the proven potential to make money. The local food economy is looking up. (And my alternative vocation, newspaper journalism, isn't.) For better or worse, Barack Obama made arugula a household name. But even before lettucegate, people were getting hooked on the idea of open-air farmers' markets with tie-dyed tomatoes and pasture-raised poultry.

It's not surprising that, in these uncertain times, Americans are increasingly craving a personal connection with the farmers who grow their food. Like passenger trains and Thanksgiving, farms occupy a particular place in the American heart. They ferry us back to the time when our predecessors staked out small squares on a vast, wild continent—when neatly tended crop rows were the only thing standing between a settler and his own mortality, between conquering and being conquered.

But farms are romantic even without the sense of history. As a microcosm for life's greatest dramas—birth, death, love, the struggle against insurmountable odds—the farm is hard to beat. Consider the childhood classics: *The Yearling*, *Old Yeller*, *A Day No Pigs Would Die*. In each, a farm forces the question of what it means to become a man. But if you dig a bit deeper, the stories aren't just about boys growing up. The act of farming requires an examination of humanity, a delineation between us and other, civilization and the natural world. In two words: self-definition; in three letters: art. And like poetry, farming is an ancient choice but a fluid line, granting each new generation both heritage and a unique personal challenge.

Where there's art, science is never too far off. And if a farmer is something of a poet, he or she is a scientist, too. A true interdisciplinarian, a farmer manages ecosystems for personal benefit and must grasp the practical applications of population-resources theory, meteorology, biology, chemistry, and ecology. Scientists should thank farmers more often: a layman's understanding of artificial selection paved the way for Darwinian theory and the modern field of genetics. Long before biologists realized the potential of genetic cryopreservation, farmers preserved the population diversity of plants and animals through hundreds of years of intergenerational commitment.

And while it's an extremely unworldly thing to say, something about the farm is quintessentially American. Farms embody the can-do work ethic that's so near and dear to our capitalist, American selves. The farm always looks forward, sacrificing long hours in anticipation of a good harvest. It knows what's important: on a farm, worth is judged not by where you start, but by where you end up. A runt chick is valued if she grows up to be a good layer; a poor layer, beautiful though she may be, ends up in the stew pot. And there's something in it of American stubbornness, too—a small, well-rounded farm says, "Trucks may stop in their tracks, cargo ships may drift in the sea, grocery stores may shutter their doors, but that won't stop my hens from laying, my orchards from fruiting, my corn from ripening."

That sort of stubbornness gives me hope.

Still, at first, the idea of our *own* farm was the kind of thing Emmett and I only whispered about in bed at night, half-afraid that it would sound too romantic in daylight, too ridiculous if we uttered it while wearing clothes like the responsible people we pretend to be. I should note that at the time of said whispering, our bed was actually a futon mattress in the back of a 1989 Toyota minivan, and I had only two pairs of pants and one rainbow-striped skirt to my name. Over time, though, even in broad daylight, the idea started sounding—well, not exactly *smart* per se, but not exactly crazy either. With a little bit of help and a lot of luck, it just might work.

Emmett's father is in the grape-growing business, and he had recently ripped out two acres of old vines. The space wouldn't be replanted until spring, and in the meantime he offered it to us. We could test-drive the organic farming life for a year, before making a long-term commitment. In our spare time, Emmett could help out his dad and I could write. (Nobody—except maybe Emmett's dad, who was too kind to mention it—realized then how little free time the farm would leave us.)

After the idea solidified sufficiently to be spoken aloud during daylight hours, we began mentioning it to family and friends. Although I braced for disapproval ("You went to grad school for *what*? I thought you were going to be a journalist!"), I was met with a host of well-wishers: My hippie grandmother dubbed starting a farm "a fan-fucking-tastic idea." A neighbor offered an environmentalist's stamp of approval, saying, "This town needs more people like you—ready to work out the best local food production system." Other friends, getting a bit ahead of themselves, vowed to come visit for our glorious end-of-season harvest party. Even my mother, who approves of very little, gave her blessing—after encouraging me to buy a farm with a guesthouse so she could visit. Oh, and by the sea, so her allergies wouldn't act up.

Armed with good intentions, two master's degrees in environmental science, and what at the time seemed like considerable farming experience (one year organizing educational food gardens, three months of a work-trade program, and four months of working on farms in exchange for room and board), Emmett and I set off to start our own farm. We didn't exactly end up with an ocean view, and our farm income won't afford a guesthouse anytime soon. (Actually, we're more or less living in Emmett's parents' guesthouse.)

Broadly speaking, the farm nestles on the floodplain of a small valley, surrounded by rolling, oak-spattered hills and Northern California's coniferous coastal range. On the outskirts of Healdsburg, Foggy River Farm's approximately two acres more specifically sit between Eastside Road and the Russian River. (When we named it, we didn't know it was going to be one of the hottest summers on record—and that smoke, not fog, would most frequently cloud our sky.) The farm is framed by Emmett's family's vineyard, and if you walk up the hill from Eastside Road a little, you just might be able to squint and make out one higgledy-piggledy postage stamp of staccato vegetation next to three skyscraping poplar trees in the midst of hundreds of acres of clean, continuous, perfectly parallel grape rows. That's us.

And this is our story.

Chapter 1:

BABY GREENS

· ·

Lettuces

It was 10:00 a.m., and I was not a born salesman.

Standing behind a rickety card table, I found myself wishing for a hole to crawl into—preferably one with a comforter, pillow, and foam-topped mattress. Or perhaps a giant tractor beam could split the sky and I'd find myself transported to a Hawaiian beach, or at the very least to Berkeley, where rumor has it the customers actually value hole-pocked produce. (They consider it proof-positive of organic growing practices, as well as evidence of superior flavor: if the bugs like it, it must be good.) There, my bumbling excuse for a farm would be prized and coddled—not given the stink eye by customers who immediately bustled on to bigger and brighter stands.

We were tucked at the end of a long farmers' market row in Windsor, California, standing behind a borrowed card table covered with a borrowed checkered tablecloth beneath a borrowed cream canvas umbrella. On the table rested a few clear plastic bags filled with two different types of mixed greens.

The bags we purchased by the thousands for fifty dollars at Reynold's Packaging. The greens, I regret to say, we grew.

"Good morning," I said, fluffing the top leaves on a bag of baby brassica mix. I couldn't hide the holes that peppered the leaves' surfaces, thousands of tiny imperfections. But damned if I couldn't make the bag look pert.

The customer, a middle-aged woman in gray sweats, gave the hole-pocked greens a sidelong glance and kept walking.

Surveying my meager display of bagged lettuces and rubbing my lower back, where a low constant throb had set up shop for the past few weeks, I was reminded that it wasn't just my salesmanship skills that were lacking.

I wasn't a born farmer, either.

I grew up in suburban San Diego, culturally (if not literally) as far away from a farm as an American can get. Neither of my parents were hippies, and neither of them were in the habit of cooking vegetables or dishing up fresh fruit for supper, let alone growing such items. My mother, who became a single working mom when I was sixteen, grew things that were mildly attractive and difficult to kill, like bougainvillea and geraniums. She wouldn't even dabble in roses: too much pruning.

Until very recently, my entire agricultural heritage could have been summarized in a couple of portentous anecdotes. My grandmother was the closest thing I had to an agricultural influence. She grew parsley and carrots in terra cotta pots on the deck of her second-story apartment. Although I do remember munching impossibly tiny carrots, which somehow never got bigger than my pinky finger despite being planted in Miracle-Gro potting soil and enhanced with Nutri-Grow fertilizer, those memories are largely dwarfed by the overwhelming disgust I felt at the invasion of snails, and my grandmother's consequent joy in their demise.

Sometimes she'd scatter the pots with snail poison pellets; other times she'd go on a gleeful rampage, following the gleaming snail trails to their source. "Be free!" she'd say, chucking the unlucky invader over the deck railing to crunch on the alley below.

Then, when I was in high school, my mother put on a family gardening day. She bought gardening tools for everyone and brought home plenty of root-bound six-pack flowers from a local nursery. The plan was to beautify the narrow side yard of the house.

While digging holes to transplant geraniums, I uncovered an earthworm, which convulsed and contorted itself in a rather terrifying way. I screamed and hurled my shiny new trowel at it. Judging by my brother's shouting ("Jesus! You idiot! You nearly cut off my middle fingers!"), my velocity was good but my aim left something to be desired.

I promptly abandoned digging duty and took up weeding. After my mom chastised me for uprooting the volunteer strawberry plants ("I was in charge of weeding that patch. Did you stop to think I might have left those plants there on purpose?"), I decided I was a hopeless black thumb. I went inside to make lunch, my gardening experiment concluded presumably for the rest of my life.

If you'd told that sixteen-year-old that, in less than ten years, she'd find herself swept up in a perilous attempt to grow things for a living, she would have rolled her eyes, swallowed her last bite of Stouffer's microwaveable macaroni and cheese, and headed toward her room to lock the door and turn up the punk radio.

Yet by some strange twist of fate, I had ended up here: perched behind a farmers' market stand of my own creation, self-consciously adjusting lettuce bags and greeting potential customers. Gone was my high school society of scorn and skepticism; gone, too, the ardent intelligentsia of my undergrad and grad school years. I was no longer part of a buzzing newsroom, driven by impending deadlines and ringing phones. Around me were my new people: colleagues, competitors, and co-conspirators in the local food system. I hoped I didn't look as out of place as I felt.

．．．．．．．．．．．．．．．．．．．．．．．．．．．．

A few minutes after the opening of the farmers' market, I left Emmett to tend the stand and took a stroll down the aisle to assess our competition. From previous visits, I'd gathered that there were two main categories of farmers' marketers: the entrepreneurs, who grew efficiently and marketed themselves slickly; and the "real" farmers, who enjoyed growing their product but didn't give a rat's ass about selling it. They seemed to prefer the joy of complaining about lack of sales to the joy of, you know, actually selling stuff. Some farmers straddled the two categories; others were a two-part business, a terse male grower who focused entirely on the production side, and a congenial wife who lovingly arranged the produce into a customer-ready array.

Grumpy Man, our kitty-corner neighbor, was perhaps the only person who fell purely into the rat's ass category. As I walked past his stand, he muttered from inside his VW minivan. Later in the season, I'd catch him drinking whiskey behind his stand. And while I never caught a whiff of the potent leaf at the market, he'd openly sell opium poppies to anyone savvy enough to recognize them as such.

Next to Grumpy Man, The Grocery Store—run by a Hmong family who carted their produce in from the Central Valley—burst with things that couldn't possibly grow in Sonoma County. Like tomatoes, this early in the season. Gnarled ginger piled high. Not to mention thirty-five other varieties of produce. They had the whole alphabet covered, with enough quantity of each product to supply two or three Windsors—from asparagus, broccoli, chard, and daikon, to zucchini and zebra tomatoes. This stand constituted a source of resentment among the truly local farmers, and a source of delight among local consumers who were thrilled to have out-of-season produce and the feel-good buzz of shopping at the farmers' market, too.

A bit further down the aisle I came across the farmer version of Cindy Crawford. Chatty, blonde, beautiful, and surrounded by a gaggle of gawking customers, she was passing out plastic bags hand over fist to customers snapping up pounds of asparagus. I immediately placed her in the first category: someone with marketing savvy who probably hired a crew of workers to grow her produce. (Later, I'd learn that Farmer Cindy actually cultivated two acres all by herself, grew the best corn in the county, fed a nearby prison with her produce, and was a practicing CPA with a master's degree in accounting to boot. So much for first impressions.)

These were my new people: vendors who stood alone behind tables brimming with strawberries, nectarines, garlic, onions, potatoes, chard, kale, and flowers. I trotted back to our stand and slipped behind the card table.

"Goooood morning," I tried again, flashing my best friendly farm-girl smile. Come on, people, I'm wearing *overalls*.

I glanced back toward Farmer Cindy's bounty and winced at the comparison. Somehow, it had taken two people to produce our meager showing of battle-weary greens. Other ingredients that went into this sorry display: six hundred hours of labor, $1,260.52 in savings, and one and a half disasters.

....

I had received news of the first disaster over the phone: the seedlings were dead.

"Which seedlings?" I'd demanded.

"All of them."

"*All* of them?"

"Well, most of them, anyway."

At the time, I was sprawled across a bed, cradling a phone to my ear. Since I was about to move to Emmett's hometown for the foreseeable future, I'd been spending two weeks with my family down south while Emmett broke ground on our farming enterprise up north.

In early May, the California summer was in full swing. I'd join Emmett in another seven days. In the meantime—when he wasn't sowing seeds, laying irrigation pipe, hunting for manure, or double-digging rows in the field—he'd been keeping me updated with daily farm progress reports via phone.

"What do you mean, *most* of them?" My mind raced trying to calculate the potential cost of this loss.

From the start, I'd been a strong supporter of extravagant seed purchasing. Part of our business plan was to offer a wide variety of heirloom produce—the sort you can admire for its unusual beauty, enjoy for its unique flavor, and feel good about, too, knowing that your dietary choices are encouraging greater crop diversity. Anybody can buy orange Imperator carrots from the grocery store; we'd offer the discerning customer carrots in every shade of a San Diego sunset. Sure, we'd carry run-of-the-mill green beans, but we'd also bring in burgundy and yellow ones. We'd plant a few standard russets, but most of our potato crop would possess purple flesh. Our greens mix would brim with flavor and spice, courtesy of succulent baby brassicas: mizuna, arugula, Russian kale, mustard greens, and tatsoi. Heck, the biodiversity of a square meter on our farm would rival that of a rainforest.

It was precisely this pro-diversity mentality that led me to orchestrate an online seed spending spree. Ten types of tomatoes? Better make it twenty. Six varieties of winter squash? I suppose that's enough, but only because we seed-saved others last year. Lacinato kale, Temuco quinoa, Mei Qing bok choy, Armenian cucumber: the more, the merrier.

Even if we hadn't previously grown these varieties from seed ourselves, we'd experienced all of them on the various farms we'd worked on over the past couple of years. And weeding someone else's kale patch is kind of like growing it from seed, right?

Our first round of spending set us back $150 at Seeds of Change and $120 at Johnny's Seeds. Then, realizing we'd forgotten some old favorites, we went back and ordered more.

To make matters worse, throughout the virtual seed selection process, I'd been the mascot cheering our team onward. With my Southern California upbringing, shopping was one skill I brought to the table. As Emmett cringed entering our credit card number yet again, I was by his side murmuring, "Remember, honey, it's an investment." While Emmett's mind was fretting over vanishing dollar signs, mine was delighting over an imaginary harvest basket that carried quinoa, leeks, heirloom tomatoes, Genovese basil, kale, corn, crookneck squash, and big, rose-petaled heads of lettuce, all at the same time. And although I knew that we were a bit out of season to start some of these plants, deep in my heart I always assumed that the investment would pay off. Or, if not pay off, at least not wither and die before ever making it into the ground.

But there's a risk of crop failure associated with any farming endeavor. Add to that the fact that we were getting a late start on the farming season. (Emmett was starting our seeds in a makeshift greenhouse in May because the field wasn't yet irrigated or amended.) And then, of course, there's the come-uppance factor. Although we'd both spent a fair bit of time on farms, neither of us had ever started, from scratch, a farming operation of this scale.

Evidently, we failed to harness beginner's luck.

More specifically, Emmett overwatered the seeds. This led to fungal growth on the roots—a type of "damping off," which is gardener-speak for anything (other than animals) that stunts and/or kills baby plants. It's hard to blame him, really. If you combine hundred-degree May weather with a busy man working fourteen-hour days, overwatering isn't exactly surprising.

"They've been struggling for a while," Emmett said. He let out a small sigh that wheezed into my receiver. "I didn't want to tell you until I knew they were really gone."

Just what I wanted to hear: no hope. Three hundred dollars' worth of seeds gone, *really* gone. Think of how much Northern Californians would have paid for local, fresh Cherokee Purple tomatoes. Or Green Zebra, or Black Plum, or that Waltham butternut squash.

With Emmett's pronunciation of doom, our conversation— like our nascent farm—didn't really seem to be going much of anywhere. After a few moments of awkward silence, we dutifully recited our long-distance I-love-yous and hung up our separate phones with a considerable amount of relief.

That night, I dreamt of seedling armies marching together. Right before I woke, every single little hopeful green thing was flattened by a team of giant red lawnmowers.

. . . .

I rose, slightly befuddled, with a purpose: time to close the communication gap in this partnership and count the casualties. I called Emmett and with forced cheer and a hearty dollop of delicacy, I inquired more specifically about our losses.

Conclusion number one: the beans rotted. As in, some of the seeds never even emerged. A post-mortem conducted by Emmett in the hoophouse—knee-high PVC pipes bent over rebar and covered with plastic in Emmett's parent's backyard—revealed that they had simply disappeared, composted in situ. Only 2 out of 216 survived. The trauma left them stunted, their ultimate fate still unclear.

If the beans fell to a fast massacre, the 330 tomatoes were victims of a slowly spreading epidemic. Some of them died quickly—now just a dehydrated wisp on top of the potting soil—but many of them lingered, cruelly prolonging our hope. Still, the stems looked a bit pinched at the bottom ("damped off," perhaps?), and although they were three weeks old, not a single plant had donned a second set of leaves. Emmett didn't harbor much hope for them.

Other casualties: 550 multiply planted cells of lettuce, 100 cells of spinach, 100 chard, 60 kale, 36 fennel, 90 arugula, 120 golden beets, 100 leeks, 50 broccoli, 24 basil, 24 cilantro, 12 sage, 12 dill, 24 chives, 24 parsley.

Tabulating the totals on a spreadsheet, it seemed safe to conclude that they added up to a small farm. A small, stillborn farm.

· ·

On the plane ride up to Sonoma County, I sat next to a friendly fellow who could scarcely contain his delight when he learned that I was moving up to the area.

"If you like food," he said, "you'll love it here. People here really appreciate good food."

"Well, I'm planning on growing some," I said, putting on a brave face. "So I hope you're right!"

Sonoma County, long a Mecca for wine lovers, is on the front lines of the local food movement. It's not a bad place to start a small farm: Healdsburg sits at the confluence of three different local Slow Food convivia. The farmers' market has been going strong since 1978. Artisanal food shops and locally sourced restaurants (the type with big plates and little foods) dot the town square. And the nonprofit direct farm marketing organization Sonoma County Farm Trails has received national acclaim for tasty, tourist-friendly farm fare. Founded by a plucky group of local apple farmers, it's been in business since 1973.

My seatmate was thrilled that I was on the brink of diving into this culture. He couldn't believe I was going to start a farm, and he described in great detail the artisanal cheese baskets he received on a weekly basis. He encouraged me to branch into the cheese market, after my farm got established of course, because cheese is so complementary to the area's wine tourism.

At this point, in spite of the seed disaster, I'd regained my farming optimism. Chalk it up to a few days spent surfing and the fact that the conversation took place a few thousand feet above the glowing Sierra Nevadas. When he suggested cheese, I wasn't thinking *if only*; I was thinking, *Heck, maybe we could get a few goats and make a little chèvre.*

As we stowed our tray tables, straightened our seat backs, and began to descend, I peered out the window. The plane was banking over the hills that had led Emmett in his childhood to fashion bows and arrows out of saplings and build wigwams out of eucalyptus limbs. He was a hunter-gatherer; although he was really successful only at gathering soap root (a bulb that is chock-full of saponin compounds and lathers like soap), he had long-term plans of growing up to be a Native American. If that failed, he figured he could always become a standard-grade hermit. And so he practiced for his eventual vocation by building shelters in the hills, sleeping in them, and constructing elaborate snares and traps—swim-in fish baskets sunk in the pond, leg snares laid across deer trails—that never caught anything. He shot arrows that didn't wound a single animal. But his failure as a hunter didn't turn him into a cultivator; on the contrary, he bristled when he was branded "farmer boy" in elementary school. He rode in the passenger seat of the big flatbed truck with his dad at harvest time, honking the horn and dropping tons of grapes off at various local wineries. But beyond the occasional truck ride and the familiar chore of dumping the kitchen compost into the compost pile, Emmett had little to do with farming.

When we first started dating, I asked him where he would live if he could live anywhere. He told me he had never thought of living anywhere but Healdsburg. At the time, he made it clear that our relationship could change that assumption—and that perhaps he just hadn't ever taken the time to consider alternatives—but there I was, flying over his hills.

"Beautiful, eh?" my seatmate said. He leaned over me to look out the window and grinned.

To my neighbor in the aisle seat, and to Emmett, the hills were a signifier of home. To me, they were just hills, the oak trees foreign, the open space perplexing, and the general appearance—from this height, anyway—not unlike a bunch of broccoli florets glued to a series of upside down colanders. In the six years since I had left my hometown of San Diego, I'd become something of a wanderer. I hadn't lived in the same house for longer than nine months, and I wasn't sure I had that kind of signifier anymore. It had once been the ocean yielding to San Diego's Mission Bay, but no longer.

As the plane banked over my future home, I knew there was water somewhere thirty thousand feet below me, but it was murky and fresh, predictable. It lacked the salt sting, the force of wave energy built up over thousands of miles of blank ocean, and the frigid upwelled deepwaters that push you under and strip you clean.

"Yes, it is," I said, my stomach tightening a little.

On the way out the door, my seatmate introduced me to his wife, who'd been sitting across the aisle from us.

"She's just moving to Sonoma County," the man informed his spouse.

"Oh really! What brings you here?" she asked. I'd just spent the past half hour explaining the whole complicated situation to her husband. How to cut the description short?

"A man," I said, and it was the first time I'd admitted it so openly to anyone, including myself. Sometimes the security of strangers can do that to you.

"Me, too," she said, smiling and glancing at her husband. And in that moment I felt a sudden pang of claustrophobia: I wasn't *really* putting down roots, was I? Shit, I'm, like, so way too young for that.

And with that I walked down the thin metal steps onto the tarmac and into a cool Sonoma County evening.

The Sonoma County airport is so tiny that it doesn't actually possess a real conveyor belt baggage claim. The "baggage claim" sits outside, a few yards from where the plane has pulled to a stop. It's somebody's job to lift each piece of baggage, by hand, into a metal display chute where suitcases pile up dangerously. I watched nervously as someone tried to wiggle a duffel out from underneath roller bags stacked three high. Note to self: not in San Diego anymore.

I looked around—where was he?—and caught sight of Emmett walking through the one-room airport. We were filled with silly back-together-again joy as we grabbed the luggage and headed out to my Subaru.

In the station wagon, our cat crouched nervously on a headrest. A little card, along with a bag of homemade cookies, perched on the passenger seat.

"Welcome home," the hand-drawn cover read. I opened the card, "By which I mean, to your cat, your car, and your man." A sweet thought—and who could ask for more than a skinny, tall, goofy, stern, wholly well-intentioned cookie-baking man—but it had been a long time since I'd had a home, and the closest thing I had to a home landscape was the mutable ocean. Ironically, the sea grounds me, and I feel little connection to the earth except where it falls away. Each time I returned to San Diego, the city felt more distant—the storefronts changed, new developments sprawling across canyonland and another lane added to the freeway—until it was entirely unfamiliar. I wasn't sure whether the sting in my eyes could be attributed to joy or to something less settling. To be honest, it was more than a little depressing that my home could be summarized as a boyfriend, a car, and a cat. I wanted a connection that I didn't yet feel. Still, I was comforted to be with Emmett, whatever that meant.

On the ride "home," we whizzed past classic Sonoma County scenery: endless rows of grapevines interrupted occasionally by sprawling oaks. The cat stress-panted the entire time, his face frozen into a taxidermy-like grimace. Emmett stalled the car. Twice. And we held hands with a death grip whenever he wasn't shifting gears.

Beginning the following morning, we'd be starting a farm . . . together.

. . . .

When starting and maintaining a farm, neophyte farmers face challenges. I knew that coming into this endeavor—but it's one thing to know a thing, and something entirely different to feel it. There's standard risk associated with any agricultural venture: the potential for a crop failure, the potential for loss of market or drop in price of goods. Add to that a young person's lack of experience. Between the two of us, Emmett and I had a few (nonconsecutive) years of farming experience. Some Greenhorns have more; some even graduated from a hands-on sustainable agriculture program like U.C. Santa Cruz's. Still, many of us went to university, not agriculture school.* And most of us lack what many other farmers have: twenty, even forty years of growing the same crops in the same place. While a hands-on, yearlong educational program would definitely have left me better prepared to start a farm, it still couldn't have taught me everything.

Place-specific farm knowledge takes years to develop. A long-term farmer has seen the gamut of pest population

---

*A young farmer featured in the New York Times was an Amherst graduate from the Upper East Side; his father is a foundation executive and his mother a writer. We'd later meet young farmers in our area with degrees in archaeology, English literature, and architecture.

booms and busts; she knows which are temporary and which are likely to stick. The old-timer has experienced the effects of these population spikes on various crops, and as a result is better at hedging bets. She has a long-term sense of the first and last frost dates, and how they might vary year to year. The farmer has seen drought and flood, cool seasons and scorching seasons, fire and freak hailstorms. In short, she is better equipped to gamble, thanks to an intuitive grasp of the local statistics. Gambling can pay off: if you guess right on the last frost date and end up with the season's first tomatoes, you can bet that your farm stand will be packed with eager customers willing to pay a price premium. But professional gamblers know the odds. Novices usually lose their savings to the casino.

Our roll of the dice, starting seedlings in a greenhouse in May, didn't turn out so well.

As I lay awake that night pondering our situation, I realized that we weren't just unfamiliar with the odds—we didn't even know the house rules. Not only did we lack long-term farming knowledge of the land, but we also were initiating a brand-new system. Like many Greenhorns, we weren't inheriting a smoothly running business; we were starting our own. And while we had a bit of an edge—Emmett's dad would prove to be an invaluable source of knowledge, and the use of his land and some of his vineyard equipment a serious financial boon—the ground Emmett had broken had been planted in grapes for decades. Because Greenhorns are starting farms wherever they can get their hands on some land, unforeseen consequences are to be expected. Some, having traveled thousands of miles in search of cheap acreage, will face entirely new seasons. Urban farmers may face soil contamination issues. As we grow organic vegetables in the midst of a giant grape monoculture, who knows what will go wrong? And although agricultural philosophies like permaculture, biodynamic, and biointensive offer loose guidelines for sustainable agriculture, they deal primarily in theory—and often disagree on specifics. In short, there is no one-size-fits-all physical blueprint for the small farm. Looking at our space, where do we plant the tomatoes, green beans, winter squash, lettuce? How do we set up the irrigation? Because none of the agricultural philosophers offer an easy answer, as Greenhorns, we were bound to sometimes do it the hard way.

I knew all of these things on an intellectual level. But it wasn't something I really felt yet. As Emmett woke me up way too early the following morning, visions of cornucopias still danced in my head.

Our first task was to get me up to speed. Emmett took me on a morning tour of the farm's three sections: the hoophouse, the raised salad bed, and the field proper.

Before we could grow any vegetables, we had to lay irrigation pipe and amend the soil.

By the very first stop, the cornucopias vanished, vaporized by a slightly less fertile reality. Time to step up and be supportive. Mine not to question why: As Emmett peeled back the plastic sheet to reveal the contents of the hoophouse, I didn't inquire after the silent multitudes of empty flats containing only potting soil and one or two fatally wounded seedlings. (I'd been warned, after all.)

Nor did I ask why a smallish salad bed was perched peculiarly across the road, hundreds of yards away from the main field and up a short, steep hill that distinctly lacked a path, steps, or on-site irrigation. I found this salad bed very perplexing: it required multiple cans of water to be ferried multiple times a day from a house-mounted spigot *up* the steep, slippery hill to the bed.*

Still, the visits to the seedling cemetery and inconvenient bed were but tiny tremors before the Big One.

After walking back from the inconvenient bed (down the hill, down the road, across the road, and down another hill), we arrived at Emmett's dad's shop—a staging structure for all things vineyard. We clambered into the Gator, our on-loan farm vehicle that runs like a Deere (being a city girl, I'd never really gotten that pun before, because our suburban push lawnmower—the bane of my brother's existence—instead ran like hell). With Emmett in the driver's seat, we took off down the main dirt road through the grapevines. Dust billowed up

---

*To be fair to Emmett's level of common sense, we were supposed to be living in the small house that belonged to the spigot. Had we been living in the house (which Emmett's parents own), the salad bed would have been justified. But after I arrived, we learned that the fixer-upper house wouldn't be livable for several months, during which time we'd spend approximately one hour every day making out-of-the-way trips to water a four-by-eight-foot salad and carrot bed by hand. This tiny bed would take up an inordinate amount of our time, but despite repeated suggestions that we just let it die, we never could bring ourselves to do it in—especially since it seemed to inexplicably thrive while everything else on the farm struggled to survive.

behind us and a nice breeze took the edge off the warm morning. I eagerly peered ahead, anxious for my first glimpse of the farm. Vines, vines, baby vines, vacant lot. . . .

Suddenly, Emmett was pulling off the road, and I wasn't entirely sure why.

Oh.

"It looks great!" I said, putting my arm around Emmett a little too tightly and smiling a little too widely.

In reality, it looked like dirt. A great big empty patch of cream dirt (the floodplain's special brand of cloddy clay soil), liberally striped with raw umber dirt (manure from a local dairy, trucked in and tractored over).

I had to look closely to spot anything growing. Eventually, I caught sight of some tiny green things on the right-hand side of the field. Walking over to the area, I determined that there were precisely three planted rows.

It was almost June. Most of our seedlings, besides these three directly sown rows, were dead or maimed. My heart was in my stomach, my stomach in my sneakers: clearly, we were fucked.

"It looks great!" I said again, then realized that I was repeating myself. "Nice irrigation. You did that all yourself, right?"

"I put two spigots on this one," Emmett explained, "so we can run a hose and drip tape at the same time." He smiled, pleased with his problem solving.

"Great," I said again. "Um, what are these guys?" All of the tiny plants looked the same to me: weed or heirloom vegetable, I had no way of telling the difference. At this point, I was thinking that if it was alive, it was probably a weed. But I paid attention to where I put my feet anyway, not wanting to accidentally pluck the final flight feather off our fledgling farm. Have you ever seen a baby parrot, all beak, neck, and pink nakedness? That was our dusty lot—and looking at it, I thought there was no way in hell this ugly creature was ever going to fly.

But Emmett, the proud papa parrot, was beaming over his dirt. "This is bok choy, that's arugula, and up at the end we have cilantro, parsley, and basil," he said, pointing quickly to apparently different but indiscernible sections of the near row. "That row is all beans—green, purple, and yellow. Then the far row's got your beets—golden, Chioggia, and the classic—along with radishes, kale, and chard."

Somehow this wasn't how I'd pictured our farm. Where were the neat rows, the worn paths, the cute barn, the sense of place and purpose? While Emmett had enthusiastically talked about the farm as our "market garden," I could think of it only as The Patch. And when I thought "patch," my connotations were less folksy pumpkin paradise, less denim-clad scarecrow, more unspoken parenthetical (of dirt).

Looking down a row of impossibly tiny alleged beets, it occurred to me that what I really needed was a rewind button. Let's go back a few hours. How about a leisurely breakfast in bed? Brunch at the omelet place in town? Then maybe Emmett could butter me up a bit by describing The Patch as a blank slate, a place with lots of potential, a page waiting for its pen, or some other crap like that.

But omelet brunches were part of our old lifestyle, the lifestyle where we had two solid incomes with health insurance plans and end-of-year bonuses. My savings account didn't cover omelets. Emmett, although happy to show affection and engage in the occasional ridiculously romantic act, is not a sugar coater. And no one writes with pens these days, anyway.

Time to buck up. "Well, it will be fun to plan all of this space out," I ventured.

"We'll plan later," Emmett said. "We've got some digging to do."

. . . .

I don't know if I'd ever felt the fear of God before, but that day, I did. Faced with a nothing of a farm, a rapidly diminishing savings account, and no employment leads, I worked *hard*. I tried to think positive thoughts about tomato jungles, bean forests, and squash thickets, but my mind kept slipping back to the empty flats of deceased seedlings. Fortunately, there wasn't too much time to think—it took considerable concentration to make my weak shoveling muscles follow orders.

We heaped manure into seven twenty-foot lines and adjusted them for straightness. Then we dug each row out by hand, turning the manure into the cloddy clay. Once each row was dug, we poured a line of soil amendments onto it, then hoed them in. The alfalfa meal, soft phosphate, ground mussel shell, and kelp meal all had to be poured separately, and each triggered a separate allergic reaction. By mid-afternoon, I was sneezing in sets of five and my eyes were watering fiercely.

We punched holes in black drip hose, then pushed red nipples into the holes until my fingertips were numb, indented, and no longer able to complete the task. By the time the rows were finished, and trenches were dug for future sowing, I was exhausted. And yet—despite my chronically itching nose and drip-irrigation eyes—a feeling of vague satisfaction crept up alongside my general state of scared shitlessness as we boarded the Gator and drove off.

It occurred to me that never before had I held a job this tangible, one where I could glance over my shoulder as I drove away and actually see the results of my labor.

....

We sat down at the dinner table that night to plan out our field and assess our options, which were diminishing approximately as rapidly as our savings accounts. We spread our beautiful heritage seed packets out on the table and scrutinized the information on the back. As one packet after another cited maturity times of 60, 75, 90, and even 120 days, we realized that we'd have to abandon visions of decadent cornucopias for the time being. By the time any of those crops were ready to sell, the farmers' market season would be half over and we'd be mired deep in farm debt. But baby greens—with a maturity time of twenty-one to thirty days—could, perhaps, pinch hit until the stars of the season deigned to show up.

Emmett had already planted one bed of baby greens half in brassicas, half in lettuces. We'd plant another right away, and one more a week later. In other ASAP crops: radishes, arugula, spinach, chard, and kale. After these were safely in the ground, we'd turn our attention to tomatoes, cucumbers, melons, peppers, and the like.

Baby greens were in short supply at the market, so we hoped that our bags, though few, would sell fast. Oh, how we doted on those greens. We mixed extra alfalfa meal into the soil to ensure a plentiful nitrogen supply. We broadcast the seeds by hand, and tamped down the soil by gently massaging it with our palms. We purchased and installed a series of micro-misters to provide the finest, gentlest watering experience around. We misted them thrice daily, and when the temperatures stretched above 100 degrees F, we brought them plastic shade cloth, an exorbitant expenditure at two dollars per foot, and stretched it over PVC hoops above the greens row so that the baby greens wouldn't be singed by the sun. We monitored them daily for any obvious weeds. And when our second, half-disaster struck, we hovered over the bed for hours trying to squish the insects that were poking thousands of tiny holes in our thousands of tiny plants.

As the day of our first market drew near, it became clear that we would have to start out as the salad stall. The bug-munched salad stall. Aside from radishes (which the seed packet noted were "a good choice for kids to grow"), our sales inventory consisted entirely of hole-pocked mini lettuces, tiny tatsoi, itsy bitsy mustard leaves, doll-sized kale, and pretty much anything else that was small, green, and decorated with pin pricks. Since we were about to rely entirely on baby greens for our initial farmers' market sales, it was time to bone up on my lettuce smarts.

Rumor has it that the English word "lettuce" comes from an Old French word, *laities*, meaning milky—probably referring to the milky white sap that comes out of mature lettuce stems after the farmer snips off the leaves. Like milk, these leafy greens have a long tradition of popularity. Lettuce dates back at least as far as the sixth century before Christ when Persian kings dined on fresh-cut leaves at their banquet tables. By the first century after Christ, at least twelve different varieties were known to the Romans. Note that none of these were head lettuces, but rather loose-leaf varieties; head lettuces didn't come onto the scene until centuries later.[6] By the early years of America's independence, Thomas Jefferson was growing fifteen varieties of lettuce in his gardens at Monticello.[7]

Fast forward to the twenty-first-century United States. Today, lettuce is a common household item and has the highest production value of any U.S. crop. California and Arizona account for approximately 98 percent of all domestic lettuce production—and, surprisingly, nearly all head lettuce sold in the United States is actually grown in the United States.[8] That's

Our first cash crop: baby greens.

in large part because lettuce can be grown year-round here. If you go to the grocery store and pick up a bag of precut, prewashed lettuce any time from April through October, it probably came from the Salinas Valley in California, just east of Monterey. If you buy that same bag any time from November through March, it came from Yuma, Arizona, or the Imperial Valley. (Huron, California, typically fills in the seasonal transition periods.) This, truly, is food as business—a smoothly operating machine offering consistent supply and quality.

And then there was The Patch, which offered neither consistent supply nor quality.

The big baby lettuce operations, like Earthbound Farms, plant each variety of lettuce separately and then combine the different types after harvest to create that lovely mix of green and red tints. We planted a seed mix so that all the lettuces grew together in a dense, biodiverse rainbow bed. Often, the faster growing varieties outpaced the slower ones, leaving us with giant green leaves and teensy red ones. The big farms specialize in multi-acre swaths of one crop, providing a single type of food for thousands of Americans. We grew a row of lettuce immediately surrounded by chard, beets, carrots, and potatoes to provide an entire meal for a few local families. They plant with ever-evolving machines; we used a more time-tested method: a rake and our hands. The big farms employ laser-leveled planting beds so that their harvesting machines can cruise over and scoop up baby leaves with precision.[9] We weren't so technical; that first market morning we snipped the leaves with scissors, our hands automatically adjusting to the depressions and hills of our uneven planting bed. The big players store their lettuce just above freezing, at 98 percent humidity, with a two- to three-week shelf life.[10] They typically inflate their lettuce bags with noble gases to prevent oxidation and enhance freshness. We plopped our lettuce in a cooler surrounded by run-of-the-mill troposphere until it made its way onto the market table and into a basket, where—if hand-misted with a spray bottle—it might stay fresh for a couple of hours. The California lettuce industry harvests more than 40,000 acres of loose leaf lettuce in a single year.[11] So far, we had planted about forty square feet. The industry earns about 300 million dollars annually,[12] but at that first market, we made, oh, fifty dollars on lettuce sales. Depending upon whether you're a pragmatist or a romantic, you might describe our tenderfoot farm as either dinky or spunky. Either way, it's safe to say we were a well-intentioned-but-muddy drop in the far larger bucket of efficient, effective commercial agriculture.

So there I stood at the farmers' market, neither salesman nor farmer, but something closer to a half-deflated idealist. One with nerdy, grandiose signs lording over her piddling produce.

What seemed like a good idea the night before—when we were wracking our brains for something, anything, to sell—looked ridiculous next to Farmer Cindy and The Grocery Store. In permanent-marker bubble letters, we'd labeled the common rosemary pilfered from Emmett's parents' garden as "Fresh Seasoning, Rosemary: For baking with potatoes, chicken, and salmon." Never mind that the stuff grows along half the sidewalks in Northern California and we wouldn't sell a single stem.

And yet somehow, over the course of three hours, customers started buying things. One at a time, haltingly at first—and then, miraculously, we actually had a small *line* forming in front of our paltry stand. Maybe they came out of pity, maybe out of curiosity, but hey, a buck's a buck. And besides, we were the only ones at the market with bagged salad. It couldn't all be pity.

At the end of the day, we counted our earnings: ninety-eight dollars, minus 10 percent for our stall fee.

"How'd you kids do?" Grumpy asked as I carried my envelope to the market manager.

"Not bad," I said.

"That's actually pretty good," my fifteen-year-old brother, Bobby, said. (We dragged him to the market with us; in town on a visit from San Diego, he was more likely to be found behind a computer than a card table full of organic greens.) "If you divide it by three, that's thirty bucks an hour."

This cheered me considerably—my salary was downright respectable!—until Emmett, ever the practical one, pointed out that it wasn't just the hours I'd spent selling; it was the hours I'd spent sowing, watering, weeding, and transplanting. And the hours *he'd* spent sowing, watering, weeding, and transplanting.

We'd touched each lettuce leaf at least five times before placing it on the table. Once when it was a seed, hand-scattered into a bed, massaged with the back side of a rake, and palm-pressed into the soil. At least three times when I'd pulled out the weeds threatening to choke it: tendrils of bindweed, wild mustard sprouts, and prickly scotch thistle seedlings. Then again when it was hand harvested, snipped leaf by leaf, and placed in a harvest bin.

And when you add those hours in, my wage was substantially less impressive: $0.13 an hour if you omit the investment; –$1.95 per hour (yes, that's negative) if you consider the money we'd put in up front.

As we broke down the card table and packed up the station wagon, Emmett shared a joke.

A farmer wins the lottery. A reporter asks him, "What will you do now that you have all that money?" The old, weather-beaten man stares into the distance, turns back to the reporter, and without a hint of irony says, "I suppose I'll keep farming until it's all gone."

Chapter 2:

BUNCHES

· · · · · · · · · · · · · · · · · · · ·

Chard, Kale, and Bok Choy

I stood at the farm stand, jaw set, and imagined my market-ing pitch. It wouldn't be in my voice, of course: the words would boom out approximately one octave lower in that brassy, gravelly made-for-radio tone that has always reminded me of a trombone.

Move over, Whole Foods.

The Foggy River Farm market stand is back and bigger than ever. Not to mention we're fresher, cheaper, and way more local than you—but while we're bigger than before, we're still intimate and friendly. If customers want to know how and where their food was grown and harvested, all they have to do is ask us, the farm-ers who grew it. How was it grown? Completely naturally, using only the finest locally sourced soil amendments and no pesticides. Where was it grown? An eight-minute drive from here. When was it picked? This morning, about two hours before the market opened.

Side note to brand manager—you can see by our folksy, hand-scrawled, permanent-marker poster and hand-painted wooden sign that our marketing strategy is ten times more authentic than *yours could ever be. Your carefully cultivated artificial ambiance is our way of life. Our new table—an old door, rescued from the town dump and perched on collapsible sawhorses—says: we're here, we're real, we're farmers. Above it hangs our beautifully redundant Certified Producer's Certificate (a certificate certifying that we're farmers), and alongside that, our newly certified hanging scale, purchased for $199.35 and sealed for accuracy by the Agriculture Commissioner for $61. And did I mention that we're selling at two farmers' markets now? Healdsburg on Saturday, Windsor on Sunday. Each market's an eight-minute commute from our fields, one south and one north. How quaint and local is* that?

Really, given the chance, who wouldn't *want to shop at our little down-home stand? But let me offer one small confession: while you display only platonic ideal produce, casting aside all those leaves, roots, and fruits that harbor the slightest earthly imperfection, our produce is, um, definitely earthly. As in been through Purgatory— and maybe through a few levels of hell and back—before settling, with great, wounded weariness, on our wobbly table.*

Well, back to reality. I couldn't blame the bok choy for looking so exhausted. Our farm was under siege. Just when we'd started to chortle over our chard—having outsmarted the summer sun by abandoning the hoophouse and adopting a direct-seeding strategy—mysterious things began to appear on our plants' waxy green leaves.

And by mysterious things, I mean holes. Millions of dastardly, ugly, big and small holes. Emmett had been crouched down above fourteen-day-old greens, weeding, when he made the discovery.

"Hmmmm," he said, and there was a certain lilt to his voice that made me pause from my beet weeding.

"What's wrong?"

"Something's eating the baby brassicas."

Our battle-worn bok choy was tasty but not quite worthy
of a Whole Foods display.

I squatted down beside him. When I brushed my hand
over the soft greens, a half dozen little black things scat-
tered. Isolating one, I realized that it was an impossibly tiny
beetle, its shell black and oily, shifting and tossing off multicolored light.

I pinched a small mustard leaf between my fingers, still
green, not yet showing its mature purple. It was pierced
through with dozens of tiny holes.

Two words popped into my mind: *crop failure*. It was a
phrase I'd seen in seed catalogs. As in, "No Russian Banana
seed potatoes for 2008. Crop failure." At the time, I had
thought, "What kind of an idiot has a crop failure? Don't these
people grow things for a living? Short of a hurricane, fire,
flood, or a few tons of salt being accidentally dropped in your
field, crop failures are inexcusable. If you can't avoid failure,
get a different job, for God's sake."

In retrospect, perhaps that reaction was a bit harsh. After all, we were now facing our *second* crop failure. (And that's being generous—if you count all the crops separately, we were in the mid-twenties.) Having already killed one farm's worth of summer seedlings, as a follow-up act we had unwittingly invited a Biblical plague to destroy our interim cash crops.

The destruction wasn't, unfortunately, limited to the baby brassica mix. The bok choy appeared peppered by machine gun fire, each baby leaf scarred with dozens of tiny punctures. Ditto the arugula. In fact, all members of the brassica family that were located in the farm's main field had become heavy artillery targets.

And then there was the Bright Lights Swiss chard, whose Technicolor stems were just lengthening and broadening to support hand-sized dark green leaves. The poor chard suffered a different sort of wound. The leaves seemed to have had the life and water sucked out of them, tattered fringes left browned and shriveled on an otherwise healthy plant. But this burn seemed bug based; it appeared on all parts of the leaf's surface whether or not the leaf was directly exposed to sunlight.

Fanning out over the battlefield, I noted that our green and purple bean seedlings—only recently emerged from the ground—looked as if they too had been transplanted from some Middle Eastern garden swept up in a sudden desert storm. They were battered, torn, and full of holes.

Our beautiful produce was defaced, defiled, destroyed. Emmett mourned, I swore, and we both headed to the computer to identify our adversaries and plan our counterattack.

This wasn't guerrilla warfare: our adversaries were easily identifiable. When we stumbled across their name it was a eureka moment, albeit one accompanied by yet another sinking feeling in my stomach.

The tiny, iridescent specs that bounced off of our bok choy every time I flicked a leaf were known as flea beetles. It fit, in a painfully obvious sort of way: they look like fleas, but they're beetles. And like their namesake, flea beetles are miniscule critters that can hop many times higher than their body size. Instead of suckers, though, these critters are chewers. Tiny, repetitive chewers who poked scads of tiny holes in our formerly beautiful greens.

But could undersized scarabs be solely responsible for a crop failure? A quick bit of research revealed that our adversaries dine almost exclusively on the Cruciferae family—also known as the brassicas. It's no surprise, then, that our baby brassica mix had been attacked. Bok choy, arugula, and kale are also members of the targeted family, which explains why they, too, looked like Havarti cheese.

But tiny flea beetles poke tiny holes. There had to be a second army advancing on our crops, one with bigger weapons.

Our hunt led us to the cucumber beetle. Known to the educated as *Diabrotica undecimpunctata*, and to us as any of several four-letter words, cucumber beetles have only one saving grace: they look like green ladybugs. This might seem insignificant until you're at a farmers' market and one crawls out of a lettuce bag in front of a customer. At that point, 99 percent of customers will say something like, "Look! A ladybug! How cute, I've never seen a green one," and your butt is covered. If a cucumber beetle resembled an earwig, a cockroach, a swollen tick, or a horsefly, our sales would likely have diminished by half.

It's sheer luck that the diabolical *Diabrotica* bears resemblance to the red polka-dotted celebrity of the insect world. But good looks aside, the cucumber beetle army was a force to be reckoned with. As though it isn't bad enough to defile pristine leaves and eat giant holes through everything, cucumber beetles also transmit mosaic virus and bacterial wilt while they move from plant to plant. An insidious adversary, the bug renders the plant ugly, and then deposits diseases that may cause it to wilt and die. In the cold of winter, when the bugs go dormant, the viruses stay safely protected in their intestines until spring blossoms and the bugs thaw out enough to resume their reign of terror.

In lieu of regular pesticide use, we turned to hand-to-hand combat: mechanical management, or physical removal of the bugs from the plants. Some folks actually vacuum up cucumber beetles, dust-busting them to their doom. But because we lacked an electrical outlet, we tried the "catch and crush" technique.

This was far less fun than the alliteration would suggest. For a girl who once threw (and still occasionally throws) conniptions over earthworms, I didn't easily embrace squeezing green bug guts out of a beetle's butt. By the third or fourth bug, my fingertips were stained green and the thought of ever eating again had begun to lose its appeal. As I watched at least two cucumber beetles fly to safety for every one I was able to catch, I got the distinct impression that I was fighting a losing battle.

Besides, we were only catching the adult beetles. Chances were, the ones we were squishing that day had already mated and produced hundreds of little eggs just waiting to hatch out more evil. There was no shortage of reinforcements to replace the fallen: each spotted female lays two hundred to three hundred eggs over the course of a couple weeks. The eggs can hatch in just five days and pass through the larval stage quickly, becoming horny young adolescents in as few as eleven days. After they've reached adulthood, they enjoy a leisurely two months during which they can parade around my vegetable rows, eating my chard and hiding their godforsaken eggs under every bean leaf.

More bad news: These guys don't just eat chard and beans. They also have an appetite for a long list of other crops, including potatoes, squash, corn, cucumbers (no surprise there), melons, and over 260 other plants in 29 families.

And, of course, whatever vegetables the *Diabrotica* didn't eat were swarming with flea beetles.

Once we knew who we were dealing with, the question was how to deal with them. After our futile attempt to catch and crush all five million cucumber beetles, our next strategy was one of mitigation. (Well, Emmett called it mitigation; personally, I considered it denial.)

We ignored the disaster, continued to sow more seeds, and hoped that the pests didn't completely kill the plants before we had a chance to sell them. Then we did our best to wash all evidence of insects off of the produce during our predawn harvest on the day of market. We dumped the produce into a harvest bin, filled it with water, and rustled the produce violently to try and dislodge the creepy crawlies. Then we drained the bin and repeated the process all over again. It was awkward to try and siphon off the free-floating flea beetles before they could land on hopeful islands of baby greens, but after a couple of rinses, any extra protein was minimal enough to be unnoticeable to the untrained eye.

But these were only stopgap measures. Selling damaged produce wasn't a solid business plan; the majority of our sales were pity purchases accompanied by a sympathetic sweet nothing. "Bad year for bugs, huh?" True, a certain species of diehard locavore approves of holes in produce as evidence of nongovernmental organic certification, but those customers were few and far between in half meat-and-potatoes, half gourmet

Sonoma County. Meat-and-potatoes Sonoma County could get hole-free greens at Walmart for less money. Gourmet Sonoma County wanted palate *and* picture perfection.

And the sting wasn't just that damaged produce didn't sell well. It was also that Emmett and I had spent countless hours coddling these plants. We had improved the soil with loads of organic soil amendments and manure, carefully sowed the seeds by hand, and hunched over the sprouts plucking weed invaders until our backs ached. We were growing these greens to be beautiful, shining examples of sustainable agricultural production. We were not growing them to be prematurely destroyed by ungrateful, sapsucking, motherfucking bastards.

Environmental ethos be damned. This meant war. So much for live and let live; hello, shock and awe.

If I had been (just hypothetically speaking here) a conventional farmer, I would have bombed the living daylights out of those bugs. One of the most common beetle killers on the market is named "Adios," clearly carrying a certain Arnold Schwarzenegger machismo. Its generic name is carbaryl, and it's a known mutagen and suspected human carcinogen. Although it's legal in the United States—and is one of the most popular broad-spectrum insecticides in agriculture, turf management, ornamental production, and residential markets—it's banned in the UK, Germany, Sweden, Austria, Denmark, and several other countries. Under the Bush administration, the EPA found in a review of carbaryl's status that "although all uses may not meet the current safety standard and some uses may pose unreasonable risks to human health and the environment, these effects can be mitigated . . ."[13] In other words, "It's really dangerous, but eventually we'll figure out a way to make it less so. And in the meantime, feel free to use it."

Carbaryl, a neurotoxin, is also directly responsible for the death of fifteen to twenty thousand[14] people in Bhopal, India. To put that estimate in perspective, the upper range is equivalent to *twice* the number of American deaths caused by Hurricane Katrina, the collapse of the World Trade Centers, the war in Iraq, and the war in Afghanistan combined. The notorious Union Carbide plant that accidentally emitted forty-two tons of toxic gas in the middle of a densely populated city did so in the process of manufacturing this pesticide.

But if I found carbaryl too creepy, I could always go the nerve gas route. Malathion, another common pesticide, is a member of the organophosphate family that operates by disrupting neurotransmission—leading to convulsions, respiratory paralysis, and death. Its chemical cousins were developed to be dropped on unsuspecting enemy soldiers in World War II. Today we apply it to agricultural pests, and regularly consume food that's been bombed by nerve gas.

Frankly, I didn't want to eat food that had been poisoned, much less apply those poisons myself. The health risks agricultural workers face are considerably greater than those facing consumers. In one study, 96 percent of surveyed farm workers reported direct exposure to pesticides.[15] Over half of respondents noted that pesticides touched their skin, over half breathed in pesticide dust, and 17.3 percent had actually been directly dusted or sprayed. Sadly, the exposure doesn't end at the field. Back home, the families of agricultural workers breathe in house dust that contains seven times the concentration of organophosphates as compared to nonagricultural families.[16] Eighty-eight percent of farm workers' children test positive for organophosphate metabolites in their urine.[17] Those are health risks I'd rather do without.

But if the conventional pesticide news is dire, the good news is that there are plenty of pesticides certified by the Organic Materials Review Institute (OMRI) and approved by the USDA for use on organic farms. If we chose to go the organic route, our arsenal could have included all kinds of toxic (but present in nature, and therefore supposedly safe) substances. The more I learned about pesticides, even organic ones, the more I realized that the creativity of chemists when it comes to taking life is downright disturbing.

It takes a certain intellectual chutzpah to transform the mundane into the sinister. Insecticidal soaps are made of fatty acids and salts, in concept not terribly different from the lye-based soaps one uses to wash one's body. They sound innocuous, but chemists have learned that the fatty acids can penetrate an insect's cells, causing them to leak and collapse; when combined with salts, this leads to a nasty bout of dehydration and spells certain doom for the little buggers. Or consider Bt (*Bacillus thuringiensis*), a naturally occurring organism that can be found in soils all over the world. It just so happens that when Bt is concentrated, it acts as a poison that dissolves the cell walls of insects' stomachs until they are basically destroyed by their own digestive juices. Sabadilla, yet another of the organic options, is a sweet-sounding powder derived from the seeds of the Sabadilla lily. It's also a stomach poison that kills pests, wipes out honeybees, and burns mammalian mucus membranes. Then there's Neem, made from the seed kernel of the Neem tree fruit (a hormone disruptor); Pyrethrins, made from the cheerful Chrysanthemum flower (a broad spectrum neurotoxin); Rotenone, which occurs naturally on some tropical plants including the crunchy Jicama root (an oxygen deprivator); and Spinosad, a soil microbe first discovered at an abandoned rum distillery (a broad spectrum pesticide, toxic to bees).

These were our options. Which instrument to choose? Since I was a little leery of spraying pesticides—even organic ones—on fresh greens that would be eaten by our customers only days later,* we compromised and decided to test out an organic spray on the cucumber beetle–ravaged bean seedlings. No one would be eating the bean leaves, after all, and the plants wouldn't begin flowering and producing beans for several more weeks.

We opted for Spinosad. It wasn't a rationalized decision; we stumbled upon it at the local agricultural supply store. There it sat on the shelf, in an innocent enough white bottle. The label told us it was organic and the clerk confirmed that it would kill the bastards.

"Great, we'll take it."

Hours later, we marched into the field with our jug of concentrated organic poison, a plastic spray bottle, and a vengeance.

The instructions directed us to dilute one tablespoon of the milky white liquid with one quart of water. Emmett poured a splash into our drug store spray bottle and tilted the liquid left and right as we both peered through the plastic trying to guess at the quantity.

"Definitely a tablespoon," I finally said.

"Without a doubt," Emmett agreed, and he turned the hose on to dilute our perfect tablespoon with a quart of water. I continued to pore over the label.

Tucked under the "precautionary statements," I found the ominous warning that "this product is toxic to bees exposed to

---

*The Spinosad organic pesticide—along with others—has been approved for use on brassica and lettuce crops as little as one day before harvest.

treatment for 3 hours following treatment. Do not apply this pesticide to blooming, pollen-shedding, or nectar-producing parts of plants if bees may forage on the plants during this time period."

Truth be told, we were in the midst of a bit of a bee crisis; we hadn't seen one in the field for weeks, and we were starting to wonder who was going to fertilize our squash and cucumber flowers. I was sorely tempted to say to hell with the nonexistent bees. We couldn't hurt them if they weren't there, right? That sounded logical enough until Emmett pointed out that—since we were waiting on pins and needles for their imminent arrival—it probably wasn't best to risk wiping out the first wayfaring pioneers with an experimental application of bug spray. The red pollen carpet wouldn't be so inviting if it were laced with toxins. So, in spite of our bout of bee absenteeism, we decided that the responsible thing to do would be to wait until the sun was on its way down and the (imaginary) bees were on their way home.

Reading further on the Spinosad label, we learned that pests ingest the poison by eating leaves that are coated with it, so it would be important to spray as much of the plant as possible. We returned later in the afternoon to armor our bean plants. Our mission: wet every square inch of leaf matter. This doesn't sound so hard until you consider three important pieces of information. First, we'd planted hundreds of row feet of beans. Second, the *Diabrotica* launch their main attack from the underside of the leaf; to be sure they'd eat spray and die, we'd need to coat the top *and* bottom of every leaf. And finally, we were using a plastic spray bottle purchased for two dollars at Longs Drugs, not the four-gallon high-pressure backpack sprayer that is recommended for this sort of work.

Off I went, crouching, kneeling, and shuffling along the vacant rows of cloddy dirt, spraying the top and bottom of every leaf. I resisted the urge to drop my spray bottle and slap at the first gaggle of bugs I came to. There was no point; if they ate the bean leaves, they'd be dead soon anyway. I felt a twinge of sadistic pleasure in my power. No wonder some farmers don't think twice about dousing their fields in poison: after all, this is war.

I traded off with Emmett until we finally reached the last row. After the final leaf had been sprayed, we turned to other evening chores, like watering seedlings and pulling weeds.

Emmett filled the watering can to soothe thirsty plants while I crouched down to pluck pesky wild mustard greens. When I came to the youngest bean row, the ground was wet and the leaves were glistening.

"Emmett, did you just water these bean plants?" I shouted without looking up.

"Yeah, they haven't gotten any all day," he called back from the opposite end of the row.

After an hour-long, painstaking, back-breaking, mind-numbing spritzathon, my brilliant farming accomplice had washed away 40 percent of our work in 30 short seconds.

"You do realize that means we have to spray it again?"

At first he was silent, and then he acted like it really wasn't such a big deal. Mountains out of molehills. No problem, it just needed a quick second pass. Slightly bitter, I retreated to the scant shade of a grapevine to let *him* make the second pass.

Quick second pass my left foot. He moved deliberately, with the demeanor of a pediatrician: superficial cheer but serious assessment. He touched each struggling seedling, examined it with gentle hands, then treated every leaf with Spinosad.

As I watched the strange choreography—crouch, cock head, peer, spray, flip leaf, spray, repeat—I was reminded of something Emmett once said about music and farming. He's a songwriter; within weeks of our first date, he'd written one for me. He buried it in a CD of other songs and I was in the car alone when I heard it. If only he could have seen my furious blushing, the grin that spread from ear to ear. And although there's not much time to make music when you're a farmer, for him, growing things fulfills the same desire to thrill other human beings with something he's made.

What he told me was that farming is about creation, and there isn't much you can create these days. It's harder to get people to buy music than vegetables, and music isn't as useful to them. Music might inspire, but vegetables keep people alive. And growing things satisfies his need for expressed creativity. Emmett even compared being a farmer to being a conductor: not playing the instruments, but coordinating them, crafting the overall piece, nurturing the various sections and making sure they're playing at just the right moment. Presiding over those harmonies makes a person feel alive.

So, improbably, farming equals music. That's why Emmett wanted to be a farmer.

Which, I suppose, was partly why he was so frustrated now: this movement didn't begin on time. It was discordant. Cucumber beetles and flea beetles were everywhere. June was making May look like a sissy, pushing easily past 100 degrees Fahrenheit. By late afternoon, even shade was little help. Heat radiated off the bare earth; the air was still and dry. Inside my jeans—the only place humid enough for water to bead—sweat dripped down my thigh. And as so often happened in those days, Emmett's workaholism—his drive to orchestrate—interfered with my languor.

"This isn't quick," I called out. "I'm exhausted. And hungry. It's time for dinner. Let's go home."

"Just fifteen more minutes," he said.

"You always say that. And then you're done half an hour later. Maybe. More like an hour."

"It's not my fault there's too much to do and it all needs to get done now. Do you want the beans to die? They're barely hanging on. Do you want to be able to sell green beans at the market sometime before winter?"

Oh lord. Not this conversation again—I was too hot and bothered to deal with it. So I plotted my cheeky disruption: I stood up, trotted toward Emmett . . . and tickle-attacked.

But Emmett, who under normal circumstances would respond in kind, wasn't charmed by my playfulness. He fended me off.

"Sometimes I feel like you just treat this whole thing as one big adventure," he said. "Something you can write about."

This perplexed me—What is life if not an adventure? And what is adventure if not something to write about?—but I nodded solemnly, biting my lower lip hard to keep from smiling.

"I mean it, I'm serious," he said. "We're trying to make a living doing this and right now it's not going well. If the plants die, we won't make any money."

"I understand that. But we work seven days a week. I need a weekend, or at least one day off. It can't be life or death all the time. And besides, if we're just going to be miserable, we could make a hell of a lot more money being miserable somewhere else. Doing something else. Then at least we wouldn't be having this exact same conversation over and over again."

The sudden shift in my tone surprised him—I get irritated when he goes all paternalistic on me—but the heart of the matter was, his worry worried me. He was the one who coaxed radishes to fruition on the windowsill of his dorm room. I was the slayer of strawberries. His parents were grape growers, and his grandparents tended orchards. My parents both worked in technology and my forebears ate red meat. If mister third-generation farmer boy couldn't keep our plants alive, my black thumb wasn't about to save them.

But Emmett's agricultural heritage couldn't turn him into an instant farmer any more than my ancestry, which allegedly traces back to Sir Francis Drake, could turn me into an instant pirate. There may be something passed through our blood— I've eaten meals on bucking boats surrounded by puking passengers and never once felt queasy—but stick me in the middle of the sea with a sextant, and I'd be as lost as the next fool.

Growing a few things in pots in a pest-free bedroom is considerably different from growing a shit ton of things in pest-infested ground in a small, haphazardly laid out field. Growing up in the country doesn't provide a person with the ability to cultivate it, just like being born in New York doesn't automatically grant a person the skills to succeed on Wall Street. Familial advantages? We had borrowed a few shovels, but not much information. Vines are perennials, more like apple orchards than bean rows. They're not even susceptible to the same pests. In short, single-harvest monocrops are an entirely different industry than that of the small, diversified, directly marketed farm: the discipline specific, not eclectic; the products bulk, not niche; the branding anonymous, not personal. And of the single-harvest monocrops, viticulture is the most different of all. It's a peculiar mix of precise science and mutable poetry: tangibles like brix and petioles ultimately yielding notes of citrus and melon, undercurrents of licorice and coffee. Certainly, our broccoli would never be subject to such scrutiny.

All of which is to say: it wasn't entirely fair to blame Emmett for not knowing what the hell he was doing.

"Can it really be fifteen minutes?" I asked. "What else needs to be done?"

"I'll do my best," he said, and sighed rather dramatically. I glared. "Yeah, fifteen minutes. And we still need to water the salad bed."

As he resumed his shuffle down the row, spraying leaves in a slightly less deliberate fashion, my mind turned to other things—like, is the naturally derived insecticide he's applying for the second time truly safe? A single leaf from the oleander bush in my front yard would be lethal to an infant or child, and while that bush is completely natural, there's no way I'd call it safe. Poison is indiscriminate, taking out predatory insects, pollinators, and pests alike. On top of that, many pesticides require that the bug eat the plant you've applied the pesticide to. So in terms of aesthetic, you're still going to have holes to contend with.

Hell, I didn't know. If this stuff could save our bean seedlings from certain destruction, I guessed it was worth the one-time application. But in the future, I'd vote for saving the pesticides for dire emergencies.

Also, honey, maybe next time we could make a point not to wash the pesticide off immediately after application.

. . . .

Weeks into our war against the bugs, they showed little sign of relenting. The Spinosad spray treatment did win us several days of breathing room, giving our beanstalks a chance to shoot upwards and gain strength. But by the end of the week, the *Diabrotica* were back in full force. And the "catch

In the midst of our mitigation strategy, I soaked bok choy to rid it of flea beetles.

and crush" method didn't do anything except slightly depress our primal urge for revenge. Our bug-fighting toolbox was running low. The organic pesticides didn't stop them; non-organic ones were off the table on principle; and we'd failed to control the population "mechanically." The little devils were still eating our plants. The squash seedlings were withering; our chard was crippled and ugly; and the beans, despite their breather, were barely hanging on. We were willing to consider anything now, short of nuclear annihilation.

A new round of research revealed two new categories of pest control. The first, I'll call "wacky home brews." The second, "biological control."

As far as I could tell, for every problem in farming, there is at least one wacky home brew out there. This is what one might call the homeopathic approach to farming. For instance, I'd been advised to spread onionskins around the base of my plants to repel cucumber beetles. Or, if that didn't work, I could blend one ounce of wood ashes, one ounce of hydrated lime, and one gallon of water and then spray the mixture on the foliage. Alternatively, a combination of hot peppers, garlic, and water might do the trick.

For all I knew, these remedies could get the job done. Just because something doesn't come in a jug with a fancy label doesn't mean it doesn't work. But my dilemma had more to do with the practicality of the solution. Spreading onionskins or making wood ash brew sounded twice as tedious as spraying Spinosad on every leaf. (Besides, where would I get two hundred row feet of onionskins?) And the Spinosad experiment had been just barely within my tolerance level—there just weren't enough hours in the day for anything more complicated. Although they were probably worth a try on the home garden, I'm afraid I lacked the patience for wacky home brews on a market scale.

So I turned to biological control. It might sound like this method would involve a hazmat suit and radon detectors, but biological control can actually be quite a friendly, gentle approach to farming. The basic idea is to use natural predators to control your pests.

Although the concept sounds very hippie-dippie eco-friendly, the truth is that biological control can be used for good or for evil. If it's botched, the introduction of a foreign predator can wreak serious havoc. For example, in 1935, the Australians brought three thousand cane toads into their country to try to control the greyback cane beetle that was ravaging their sugarcane crops. To put it mildly, the strategy backfired. The grotesque toads didn't bring the beetle population into check; instead, they spread across the country, crowding out native frogs, eating honeybees, and poisoning household pets and native mammals with toxins exuded from their warts.[18] That's biological control at its worst.

So lesson number one was that we didn't want to introduce some slimy, spiky creature from across the globe to our vegetable patch with the unfounded hope that it might eat our cucumber beetles and flea beetles, because it might also eat our salad greens and poison our cat.

But we could consider something more benign and time-tested, like unleashing half a million ladybugs to gobble up all the *Diabrotica* eggs. Or perhaps we could release a fleet of soldier beetles to kill the cucumber beetles. The list of potential predators sounds like warriors plucked from a 1970s sci-fi novel: tachnid flies, parasitic nematodes, braconid wasps.

Every time I see those clear plastic boxes of live ladybugs for sale at the checkout stand of the hardware store, I'm tempted to buy one and crack the lid to watch the ladies parachute across the store on their little red wings, settling on green garden hose coils and bright red rakes, yellow seed packets and dark sacks of compost, carabiner key chains and Mars Bars. Now that I had a pest problem, maybe I had a good excuse to live out my fantasy.

Trouble is, when you release one thousand ladybugs into an unbalanced ecosystem like my field (or a hardware store, for that matter), you're lucky if one or two stick around long enough to have a light aphid snack before fluttering on to greener pastures. The bugs-in-a-box miracle I'd been eyeing was nothing more than an agricultural placebo—designed to make the home gardener feel better without actually doing anything.

But rumor has it that if you create a habitat for ladybugs—and other friendly predators—and draw them in from your surroundings, then you've got a long-term solution. (Pre-packaged predators do better when released into this setting as well.) To create a predator-friendly habitat, some farmers let wilderness thrive on the edges of their fields; some plant hedgerows of native plants in swaths that divide their fields; some design insectaries to attract good bugs with a carnival of colorful flowers. Similarly, some farmers will mix repellent plants in with their crops to keep the bad bugs away. Broccoli, calendula, catnip, goldenrod, nasturtiums, radishes, rue, and tansy are all said to fend off cucumber beetles. An alternative to the repellant crop is the trap crop: a tasty plant that draws pests away from your real market crops. For instance, an abundant row of sacrificial radishes can keep flea beetles occupied while a nearby row of cabbages matures.

Although I would have loved to plant some trap crops, or raise a hedgerow, or create an insectary, none of these would solve my short-term problem. I had too many *Diabrotica* and flea beetles eating my greens *right then*, and building up a reservoir of predators can take years. I didn't even know if we'd be on this property a year from now. And we certainly wouldn't be growing vegetables on the exact same spot; our field was destined to be replanted in grapes next spring. So, like roughly 30 percent of young farmers in the United States, we couldn't plan very well for the future because we didn't control the land we were cultivating.[19]

Back to square one. Squishing the bastards didn't work. Spraying organic pesticides only slowed them a little. We determined wacky home brews to be too time-consuming and biological control too long-term. We wracked our brains for a magic bullet.

When we finally come to a solution, it was painfully obvious what we should do—and what we should have done all along.

. . . .

"It says it *right on the seed packet*," Emmett said woefully.

"Don't be too hard on yourself. We were busy."

"We're always busy. That's no excuse."

With Emmett's discovery, we stopped thinking like Americans and started acting like Russians: we retreated and hid under blankets of white.

Obviously, there was no snow involved in a Sonoma County summer. But a floating row cover helped us disappear in the midst of a siege. Translucent enough to let 75 percent of light through while providing a physical and visual barrier to invaders, the only downside to this polyester fabric was its cost (and the fact that it would start to disintegrate after a couple of months of sun). We coughed up $40.65 at the local agriculture store for a 6-by-250-foot roll and squeezed the awkward package into our station wagon, shimmying it between the driver and passenger seats. (On our long-term wish list: a pickup truck.)

Back at the farm, we threaded a length of PVC pipe through the cardboard center. We jammed one end into the ground; Emmett held the other end while I ran the length of the field. The lightweight white row cover unspooled behind me like a giant roll of toilet paper, rising and falling in the breeze. When I reached the end, Emmett cut the row cover; we sidestepped over the brassica row and laid the white cloth down. I jogged back to Emmett, grabbed a handful of hooked j-stakes. Walking on either side of the row cover, we pierced the fabric and pressed the metal stakes into the ground, sealing the plants within—and, we hoped, the pests without.

Through retreat, we won. And confirmation of our victory came not from thousands of little beetles waving tiny white flags—although that would have been deeply, deeply satisfying—but from piles of whole, hole-free greens. Approximately one month after our first day hawking holey greens behind a tiny card table, we pulled into our market parking space with heads held high.

First things first: we murmured thanks to the goddess of knots and ropes, which had once again miraculously kept our makeshift table safely affixed to the roof of the station wagon through the curvy, pothole-pocked country roads. Then we pulled the combination of daisy chain knots (Emmett) and bowlines (me) free, set up our little stand, and made ready to present our produce.

Out of the harvest bins and onto the table came big, radiant bunches of Bright Lights Swiss chard; deep green stacks of Lacinato kale; bags full of crisp, clean bok choy and tender young arugula. All clean, hole-free, shining examples of local sustainable agriculture. In the final few minutes before market time, we ran down a mental checklist: labels out, starting cash accounted for, misting bottle handy. We were ready to sell.

As the morning wore on, we were heaped with praise for our young, tender chard—even Grumpy Man tried some, totally raw—but the crowning compliment of the day came from a customer about four feet tall, still in the Velcro shoe stage of life.

The kid was tugging on his dad's leg and ogling our basket of pristine baby bok choy. "Can we get some bok choy?" he asked.

"We can get *big* bok choy at the supermarket," the dad replied, eying the six dollars per pound price tag and trying to move his son onward.

But the boy would not be moved. "Pleeease," he begged, yanking harder. "I love bok choy!"

The dad looked half-embarrassed, half-proud as he retrieved his wallet. Emmett and I looked at each other without even a hint of embarrassment. The little bulbs of bok choy palely glistened. The Lacinato kale gleamed a deep shade of blue-green, unblemished and primordial.

Our greens were growing up, and somehow our short-lived farm had already gained a sense of history, or what history should be—one generation learning from the previous generation's mistakes.

Chapter 3:

DARLING DODOS

· ·

Pre-Eggs

At 7:35 a.m. on our one-day "weekend"—a shovel-free Thursday that I'd demanded from Emmett after several weeks of nonstop work—I rolled out of bed and snapped open my cell phone mid-ring. Restricted number.

"Hello."

"Lynda?" a woman's voice inquired.

"Yes?"

"Your birds are here. You can come around back."

"Great! Thanks so much!"

I was so excited that not only did my words come out as a rather embarrassing girlish squeak, but I also hung up the phone right then and there without entirely intending to. Damn—restricted number; couldn't call back.

"They're here," I informed Emmett. "Let's go."

"Here where?" he asked. "Which post office?"

"There's more than one?" He nodded. "Crap."

That appropriate four-letter word was, perhaps, the final punctuation on a long-standing should-we-or-shouldn't-we debate. From the very first time we visited the farmers' markets as customers and prospective vendors—when the Windsor market manager casually mentioned a local shortage of farm-fresh eggs—my mind had been made up. We should raise chickens—thirty of them. Rhode Island Reds, White Leghorns, and Ameraucanas, starting with day-old chicks.

Emmett's main resistance to my idea had to do with our status as rootless—if not outright itinerant—farmers. What would we do with a flock of thirty chickens once we found our own land to farm? We couldn't just administer a sedative and toss them in a suitcase when moving day came. In contrast to our stoic, seasonal vegetables, these moving, breathing creatures could live upwards of ten years. And our ability to keep a future flock with us would depend on whether we ultimately settled nearby or somewhere across the country. It wasn't just the birds themselves that would require a substantial investment of time and money either. There were also the coop, yard, and fence, none of which would be easily transferable. Why put in all the work now, Emmett wondered, if we're just going to have to do it all over again a few years down the road?

It was this risk of loss that made Emmett hesitant to invest his time, money, and emotions in my poultry idea. He had a point, but when push comes to shove, I'm just not particularly risk averse. I prefer to plow ahead and deal with the consequences later—a personality trait that becomes particularly prominent when cute baby animals are involved.

After the market manager planted the idea in my head, I quickly became a pro-chicken pest, badgering Emmett with a variety of arguments to convince him that chickens would be integral and irreplaceable members of our farm. My lines of attack were manifold.

First, there was market demand. In Healdsburg, farm-fresh eggs sold for six dollars a dozen—and even at that rather appalling (to customers) price, there were never enough. The primary egg vendor would often sell out in the first hour or two. Only a few other farmers offered a small number of eggs from backyard flocks. Some, lacking the proper egg-vending permit, even sold them under the table. Eggs were so popular that they functioned as an effective marketing strategy, drawing customers to the produce stand. While customers were admiring the multicolored eggs and chatting up the farmer about her chickens, heck, they might as well pick up some tomatoes and onions for an all-local omelet. The rainbow assortments of eggs offered by local farmers were especially popular, and they were not something a person could find at the grocery store. Hence my choice of chicken breeds: White Leghorns for white eggs, Rhode Island Reds for brown, and hatchery Ameraucanas (a.k.a. Easter Eggers) to lay the much-coveted blue and green eggs. And if we bought day-old chicks—as opposed to laying hens or started pullets—we'd only be out about two dollars per bird, rather than the twenty dollars per bird that quality laying-age hens cost. Never mind that baby chicks are a hell of a lot cuter than big chickens, and are also more likely to bond with their owners.

So marketing was my first line of argument. Then there was the concept of a closed-loop agricultural system: a farm that requires no additional inputs (specifically in the form of fertilizers) in order to maintain productivity from year to year. This sustainable ideal is a particularly difficult thing to achieve because every farm, with every harvest, exports nitrogen, carbon, phosphorus, potassium, and calcium. Drawn from the soil, contained in beet bulbs, chard leaves, broccoli heads, and green beans, these essential elements are destined for customers' bellies. And what doesn't go into bone, muscle, and nervous system function ends up in the john, not back on the field.*

So how does a farmer ensure continued productivity of his soil? Although nitrogen may be replenished with the help of legumes—which snatch nitrogen from the air and deposit it into the soil through a process known as nitrogen fixation—the other elements necessary for plant growth are trickier.

Which is where chickens come in.

Foraging poultry can help narrow the gap, if not close the loop entirely. Chickens are extremely effective composters—and they're willing to compost things that wouldn't end up in a typical farm compost pile, thus providing a net influx of nutrients. Chickens are more than happy to forage for weeds, weed seeds, and bugs, turning them into mineral-rich manure. They enjoy dairy products, baked goods, and oily cooked leftovers that would normally spoil the compost pile. They'll also gulp down thinned seedlings and leftover market produce. Although chickens burn off and use up some of the compost's value through digestion, this loss is balanced by the farmer's satisfaction in feeding leftover market produce to a live, hungry creature (one who'll turn it into an egg, no less). The alternative can be disheartening: tossing beautiful bouquets of chard and kale on the ground to wilt, wither, and rot.

There are other benefits to chicken composting: it can provide a nitrogen boost midseason. While nitrogen-fixing legumes are usually planted in winter as a cover crop—and

*The recoverability of these nutrients from human waste is debatable. For a while, the New York City metropolitan area functioned as one great closed-loop agricultural system. Long Island was the farm belt that provided New York City with its food; the city, in turn, provided the farms with what was delicately termed "night soil." "Night soil"—composted human waste—is no longer considered appropriate for growing food, although some farmers use it to fertilize non-edible shrubbery around the farm.

a backyard compost pile might take a year to fully mature—chickens miraculously crap year-round. For market growers like us, who easily plant eight lettuce successions in a given growing season, it's useful to have a quick, easy soil pick-me-up on hand—one that you can add anytime, anywhere.

Another chicken benefit I pointed to: effective pest control. Chickens love bugs. And although they're not particularly discriminating creatures—they're not about to pass up a beneficial insect like a ladybug or mantis for the greater benefit of the farm—they can prevent insect populations from exploding. Besides, our farm (like most small farms that find themselves growing in the middle of a monoculture) possessed an abundance of evil insects and a paucity of good ones. If I couldn't find any ladybugs, but brushed dozens of cucumber beetles off my clothing by day's end, I guessed that the chickens would dine primarily on the green, gooey cucumber beetles.

Finally, I had a bit of a moral and culinary imperative. Emmett and I had both been vegan for a number of years. His primary reason related to health; mine, ethical treatment of animals. But while I had stopped eating eggs, I never stopped craving them. And I had a hunch that perhaps I could find a moral, ethical way to produce eggs that would satisfy both my conscience and my cravings. With a Foggy River flock, we could demonstrate to ourselves and our community the feasibility of local egg production—a model system in which chickens would roam a large yard; eat a healthy diet of organic produce, organic grains, and foraged foods; and consequently produce healthy, tasty eggs. I started salivating just picturing it: guilt-free scrambled eggs and tofu sausage on multigrain toast with Earth Balance faux-butter spread. Yum.

And so I was able to convince my farming partner that Foggy River Farm really, truly needed chickens. We set aside the challenge of what to do if we were to move to another property, and invited poultry into our current, transient lives.

The number of chickens—thirty—was partly thanks to back-of-the-envelope calculations, and partly thanks to chick shipping requirements. If thirty hens laid eggs six out of seven days, I'd have fifteen dozen eggs to sell at market, netting me ninety dollars per week. That, plus the advertising value for our market stand, would make chickens worth my time. And if we wanted to order day-old chicks from a hatchery we had to order at least twenty-five birds anyway.

For the record, I'm not the only Greenhorn farmer who became enamored with the idea of chickens. It turns out it's a common theme on start-up farms all across the country, from Oregon to Vermont to Missouri.[20]

It's not just professional farmers who raise broiler chickens and egg layers, either. Even suburbanites and city-dwellers are getting in on the action. Historically speaking, livestock is no stranger to the city. Nineteenth-century New York City streets were home to thousands of pigs that roamed the alleys and avenues eating trash.[21] Families commonly kept hogs, milk cows, and chickens for home consumption. In other words, it wasn't unusual for non-farming Americans to have one foot in the world of agriculture. But urban livestock fell out of fashion in the tidy, techno-savvy cities and suburbs of post-war America. Backyard bevies came to be considered filthy, unhealthy, and definitely not in vogue. Personally, my parents drew the line at a dog or cat. Anything bigger belonged on a farm.

But now the pendulum is swinging back, and urban agriculture is all the rage. For reasons that range from eating locally to reducing carbon footprints, more and more Americans are raising their own animal products—from backyard hens in Los Angeles to rooftop honeybees in New York City. In cities big and small, residents are raising mini-flocks of egg layers. Although some cities have ordinances in place banning back-yard chickens, many others allow them. And many of those cities with prohibitive ordinances are eliminating them in the face of populist pressure. Experts put the percentage of U.S. cities that tolerate backyard chickens at about 65 percent.[22] Big cities like Los Angeles and New York have no limit on residential chickens, so long as you don't invite any loud-mouthed roosters to join the party. In our region, the Sonoma city council has passed an ordinance allowing sixteen chickens and eight rabbits on any city parcel. Every year, more cities join the ranks of the chicken-friendly, allowing their residents to dabble in small-scale fowl raising. If thousands of urbanites with no farming background can raise chickens, why couldn't I?

Which brings me to the abject terror of picking up thirty tiny, helpless creatures from the U.S. Postal Service. The very same USPS that delivered my brother's eighteenth birthday present drenched in water, missing several key gift components, with an apologetic note at the bottom of the box essentially stating that "shit happens."

Shit better not have happened to my chicks. At 8:00 a.m., an hour before the post office officially opened (and fifteen minutes after fruitlessly searching the first, incorrect post office), Emmett and I headed around back—the one instruction I'd managed to receive from the postal worker over the phone—to the "authorized personnel only" loading area. After a few minutes of aimless wandering, we found a woman loading up her postal truck.

"Excuse me," I said, a little embarrassed, "I'm here to pick up chicks."

It occurred to me later that some women might find this suggestion offensive, but the postal worker seemed to take it in stride.

"One sec, just wait here," she said, and disappeared.

Within a minute, she returned with another postal worker who bore a peculiar package: a perforated cardboard box that was peeping rather indignantly.

"We got a shipment of crickets this morning, too," she said. "I was beginning to feel like a zookeeper."

She handed me the package. Thirty birds plus a box: oddly lightweight, just a few pounds.

"What did you get?" the first postal worker asked.

"Chicks," I said, grinning widely.

"I know," she said, smiling kindly at my idiocy. "What kinds?"

I rattled off the breeds: "White Leghorns, Ameraucanas, and Rhode Island Reds."

"Rhode Island Reds will eat you out of house and home," the woman informed me. "White Leghorns will lay their hearts out for you. And Ameraucanas will be your friendliest, nicest birds."

"I take it you're a chicken fancier," I managed.

"I used to be," the lady replied. "Now I'm a truck driver."

Not really knowing how to respond, and hoping this wasn't an omen of things to come, I bid her farewell and turned toward my station wagon.

As I gingerly placed the cheeping package in the trunk, I felt equal parts thrilled and terrified—terrified that not all of them had survived the journey from Fresno, and thrilled to be in charge of thirty baby creatures. Not to mention the inherent exhilaration involved in a bizarre experience. Picking up thirty live animals at a closed post office: definitely weird.

Dropping thirty chicks in the mail with no food or water may seem cruel, but chicks, who have recently absorbed their calorie-rich yolk sac, are well equipped to travel during their first three days of existence. In a natural setting, eggs in a given clutch hatch at different times—and the mother bird doesn't get off the nest to lead her brood to food until all of her young have hatched and dried off. Having an extra supply of calories for those first few days enables the earliest hatchlings to survive until mama's ready to feed them. So although nature wasn't setting out to aid the mail-a-bird business, genetic survival mechanisms nonetheless helped spawn a multimillion dollar hatchery industry.

Still, mailing tiny creatures isn't without peril. The little ones, lacking a hen's warmth, can get too cold and die. Often the immediate cause of death is suffocation—the birds pile together to stay warm, and the weaker ones end up on the bottom. For this reason, most hatcheries either require a

How could you not fall in love with these guys?

minimum purchase (twenty-five birds for body heat) or charge extra to send chicks in insulated boxes with chemical heating pads. And only a few hatcheries ship year-round—many close up shop for the coldest months.

Back at home, Emmett sliced through the packing tape and peeled back the lid. All thirty of the little fluff balls within were walking, huddling together, or tilting back their heads to tell me exactly what they thought about their current accommodations. Judging by the loud cheeps and fluffed feathers, they were unimpressed.

I hoped they'd find their new home more to their liking. Over the past few days, I'd readied a makeshift brooder: a ninety-quart clear plastic tub outfitted with a ventilated lid I'd fashioned out of wood and hardware cloth. The setup was floored with paper towels for the chicks' arrival and spruced up with a plastic waterer and a small galvanized trough full of chick starter (a bulk mixture of grains). A red 100-watt flood lamp rested on the hardware cloth, emitting rosy warmth. All in all, a cozy, habitable place—far more inviting than the chilly cardboard shipping box.

They were ruddy brown, pale yellow, ocelot striped—Emmett and I began to move each impossibly tiny bird from the cardboard box into its new home. As I placed each downy baby in the brooder, I dipped its beak in the water so it would know where to go for a drink. Then I peered at its rear end and released it onto the paper towel floor.

My new flock. Little did I know that, from that moment forward, each hour that passed, each time I refilled the feeder, each problem I had to troubleshoot would create another opportunity for me to fall in love with these brainless, adorable little creatures. Innocent though they were, those thirty birds would form the gateway drug for a full-fledged poultry addiction—the sort of hit that breaks hearts.

It all started with the pasty butt.

"Don't forget to check her bum," I reminded Emmett as he transferred a Rhode Island Red chick.

I'd been reading up on chick rearing, which meant I was painfully aware of all the hundreds of things that can go wrong with newly hatched poultry. Top on the list was pasty butt, a condition sometimes caused by the stress of shipping. Excrement could supposedly crust over the bird's vent, preventing it from eliminating waste. This sounds neatly scientific, but what it really means is that a new, anxious chick owner will spend the first seven days constantly inspecting thirty baby bird butts, and wiping as necessary.

Well, not exactly wiping. Since chick butts, unlike human baby butts, are festooned with feathers, extracting excrement

We checked each chick for pasty butt before introducing them to their new home.

is complicated. In the following few days, I'd employ scissors, dampened towels, warm-water chick bidets (in saucers, no less), and the "fingernail pull"—a technique that I'd eventually become quite good at. None of the books I had read on chick raising had mentioned that chick poop is like glue. On various websites, longtime poultry owners recommended removing the tiny feathers around the vent, which is where the fingernail pull comes in—but pull too hard, and you're likely to rip off tender skin, which causes a problem worse than pasty butt. Basically, the best technique of all is to pray like hell that your chicks don't have pasty butt. (And if they do, to keep reminding yourself that these are the intimate sorts of experiences that form the basis for all strong relationships. A friend in need is a friend indeed.)

"Is this pasty butt?" Emmett asked, showing me a chick.

"Ummm, I don't know."

That was our other problem: while all the books warn of the dangers of pasty butt, not one of them actually bothers to show a picture of it. Which led to Emmett's valiant attempt to pick off the chick's dried-up version of an umbilical cord—where it was connected to the yolk sac—which was located just below its vent.

"It's not coming off."

"Okay, just leave it, it doesn't seem to be getting in the way of anything. The vent's up there, not down there, right?" I pulled an Ameraucana chick in close. Her vent contracted and opened in pulses, a pink little O answering in the affirmative.

In short order, the thirty chicks were transferred into their new home. They huddled beneath the heat lamp, a solid multicolored mass of fluff: pale yellow, pinkish red, mottled and striped brown, and black and gray. Emmett and I hovered over the brooder for a few minutes, just watching—entranced as the chicks jockeyed for position, each one trying to move into the middle of the mass for warmth. A few ventured out into the greater brooder space—the biggest world they'd yet known. I almost cheered when one figured out that the trough was for food, and began pecking at the chick starter.

And then it hit me: I was hooked. And I had to admit (to myself, if not to Emmett) that the lines of argument I'd used to swing the poultry debate over to my camp were, well, somewhat beside the point. I've always had a knack for constructing convincing arguments to get what I want. (When my single mom was considering getting a gun for safety, I convinced her to get a puppy instead.) And the root of any desire usually lies far from the smoke-and-mirrors way it's expressed.

I think the real reason I'd just ordered thirty chickens was that deep down, I'm a dog person. I crave acceptance and adoration; I thrive on the sense that other creatures are relying on me. Acquiring chickens satisfied the desire for something that would respond to me, something I could mother a little. Something that might make me feel more at home in the unfamiliar landscape of Sonoma County. Something that would give me roots. (Or let me nest. Whatever.) While Emmett worried about how to keep our operation light, transferable, unbound, I was trying desperately to anchor myself to the sticky clay soil of the Russian River Valley. Even if we were to move in a year or two, I needed to feel like I owned some piece of this land if I were going to make it through this first season. And since I didn't literally own the land, at least I could carve out a space for my chickens to scratch and peck. A place for them to leave a layer of rich, fertilized soil, to take the pasture and make it into eggs. To take dirt and give me gold.

Unlike Emmett, I'm not fully satisfied by the simple joy of growth. I find pleasure in eating food I've grown, but it's not enough. Frankly, I derive more pleasure from receiving rave reviews from a customer, from the sense that my hard work has provided sustenance for another human. Emmett is a patient person and attentive; he enjoys details, and the silent, slow-growing vegetables suit him. When I met him I noticed right away that he was filled with an uncanny, quiet confidence and sense of purpose—something I didn't understand because it was so different from my need for affirmation. He doesn't speak unless he really needs to and is certain his thought will contribute significantly to the discussion. When he does say something, his sentences are well thought out. Not me; I lack any sort of filtration system between thought and speech. It runs in my family: none of us knows what we're saying until it's said.

All of which somehow seems indicative of the differences between animals and vegetables. Vegetables have a certain charm—and they do require constant attention—but when it comes to personality, they're not exactly the life of the party. Vegetables don't require the commitment that animals do; in a few months, you're done with them. You simply pull up and move on. Whereas chickens—crazy, unpredictable, needy—make the farm home.

Emmett probably understood some of this, in the way that someone you've lived with for years automatically grasps your subtext. He gamely went along with my mental math—how many dozens per week, and how much money earned? Why chicks and not laying hens? He probably suspected my hidden motivations, but he chivalrously kept his thoughts to himself.

As I watched a day-old Rhode Island Red chick tilt back her head to swallow a sip of water, I tried to convince myself that we were doing this for the right reasons.

．．．．．．．．．．．．．．．．．．．．．．．．．．．．．．

It's surprising how quickly life with thirty chicks in the garage starts to feel normal. At the farm I sowed seeds with abandon, racing through tasks and constantly pestering Emmett for the time, eager to rush home to check on the babies. When I was home, I could barely be pried away from my hover position over the brooder.

There were, of course, the midnight checks—when I tip-toed into a dark garage, groggy-eyed and stumbling, making my way toward the red glow of the heat lamp. (Hell or hearth, it's anybody's guess.) Top on the nighttime checklist was temperature: for the first week, chicks' living quarters should hover around 95 degrees F. I didn't have a thermometer, but I did have the observational ability to judge the chicks' comfort level. If the chicks were spread out across the brooder—some eating, some sleeping, distributed regardless of the location of the heat lamp—they were doing okay. If they were as far away from the heat lamp as they could get, lying down and panting, they were too hot. Huddling under the heat source, too cold. Thus far they seemed pretty happy with the temperature: once they warmed up from their USPS experience, they started careening all over their new habitat.

Then there were the morning rituals. Each day, I rose early to squeeze in some chicken time before we headed over to the field. In order to get each chick used to human contact, I hand-transferred the chicks from one ninety-quart container to a second ninety-quart container with fresh paper towel bedding. Some chicks squealed like a cat in a car; others fell asleep on my palm, basking in the radiant heat of my hand. Once that was done, I topped off the food, replenished the water supply, and watched chick TV until Emmett told me he was leaving whether I was ready or not.

Then there were the transitions of growth: from paper towel bedding, which is recommended for the first day or two while the chicks learn to identify their food, to grown-up bedding. From one container, which is big enough for the first seven days, to two containers. (And then three. And then four.)

Transitions were where the biggest hiccups occurred. Take, for instance, the seemingly simple transition to grown-up bedding. Most poultry books recommend pine shavings, approximately one inch deep, placed on the floor—it prevents feces from sticking to the birds' feet, keeps the brooder smelling fresh, and provides a textured, insulating bedding for the birds to sleep in. However, the only pine shavings I could find in the local hardware store boasted a big warning label: NOT FOR USE IN ENCLOSED SPACES: USE ONLY IN OPEN ENCLOSURES. Maybe I'm too easily scared off by the use of all caps, but I decided to go with a second option listed in one of the more esoteric guidebooks: peat moss.

So I returned home, covered the brooder floor with peat moss . . . and the chicks immediately determined it to be lunch. An internet source revealed that if the chicks ate peat moss and then drank water, the peat moss would expand fivefold in their stomachs, killing them. This spurred an emergency return trip to the hardware store to get the pine shavings, all caps be damned.

After the peat moss scare subsided, the pine shavings opened up a new world. Now the little ones could scratch the pine shavings with their feet, kick it all around the brooder, and then peck through it to find bits of spilled food (and/or eat wood, which does not expand considerably in water). The chicks lay in the pine shavings, fluffed their wings, and kicked the litter up into their feathers to take a "bath."

I found this pecking, scratching, and dust-bathing behavior to be really cute until I realized that really, it wasn't so different from having a poop-throwing monkey in the house: feces in the food, feces in the water, feces on the animals. Feces on the human caretaker, too.

These are the things the poultry books don't tell you. Namely, that you'll spend an hour a day picking chick-kicked poopy pine shavings out of the feeding trough and waterer. That you'll think you're the only person who has ever done this, that something must be wrong with the design of your waterer/feeder/litter/chicks. There isn't, of course. (Just like there isn't anything wrong with the baby who fills up diapers with poop four times a day.) It's part of the process. You can try elevating the waterer and feeder above kick-level by placing them on a two-by-four pedestal, but that just opens up a new can of worms: the waterer or feeder capsizes, which results in wasted feed or soaked litter, respectively. Soaked litter, of course, can grow toxic mold, which can kill chicks. Drenching the fecal matter also releases a powerful ammonia smell, which can harm the birds' small, developing lungs. (That, the books tell you.)

In other words, as a novice farmer, most of what I needed to know about raising poultry couldn't be found in a book or a class, or even in the spoken advice of a fellow farmer. I had to learn the hard way, by doing. I will admit, though, that I had one decidedly twenty-first-century resource at hand: BackyardChickens.com, "the #1 destination for the information you need to raise, keep, and appreciate chickens." If there's one tool available to Greenhorn farmers that our predecessors lacked, it's the Internet.

For starters, the Web didn't exist at all when today's old-timers were first learning the ropes of farming. But even now that these older farmers have home computers, let's be honest: most folks over fifty just don't have the same knack as us young'uns when it comes to getting the biggest bang for our Internet buck. The numbers support this assertion. A 2008 survey by the American Farm Bureau found that 90 percent of farmers age 18 to 35 have cell phones and computers, and 99 percent use the Internet.[23] As recently as 2009, only 61 percent of *all* farmers owned or leased a computer and 59 percent had access to the Internet.[24] So, while information technology use is growing rapidly among farmers of all ages, it is the youngest of us who have been able to hit the ground running.

This is especially true for many Greenhorn farmers, those of us who didn't go to agriculture school or spend our teenage years as apprentices on working farms. Instead, we attended colleges, studied in computer labs, researched with online databases, and used Google Books to fill our bibliographies. We grew up in front of the keyboard. To us, the Internet search is a familiar art. Rather than relying on traditional networks of farmer-to-farmer support—calling up our neighbors to ask if they have any wisdom to dispense on prolapsed chicken vents, coughing goats, or shriveling winter squash—we are much more likely to first open up a Web browser and perform a quick search.

I'm not saying that farming in the Internet age is an improvement, but I do know that it introduces a decidedly different approach to agricultural problem solving. We can pull up crop analyses from all the agricultural extension schools in the country from our living room sofas. We can look at photos of flea beetles, cucumber beetles, squash beetles, and predator beetles without even getting out of our pajamas. And in the case of chicken crisis management, we can communicate with a vast pool of other poultry people from all across the country, just by logging in. BackyardChickens.com gets a whopping six million page views per month,[25] and its online forum is fifty thousand members strong. And although the individual chicken fanciers who frequent the website probably don't have a veterinarian's grasp of poultry problems, the collective intelligence of the group rises above its component parts.

Another thing the guidebooks don't mention but my Internet queries confirmed: how quickly the chicks develop distinct personalities. Stumpy the rooster—identified by the hatchery with a pink paint dot on his head—was a sweet, mellow guy who knew all too well that he was outnumbered. He let his twenty-nine lady companions walk all over him. (He was also slower to feather out than the fems; his wings, stubby by comparison, earned him his name.) The other Rhode Island Reds and the White Leghorns remained indistinctive, but a number of the Ameraucanas earned names thanks to their distinct down patterns: fluffy, gray Penguin; friendly Bandit with her raccoon mask; small but spunky Runt with her scruffy mottled head.

And then there was the chick that quickly wiggled her dirty little butt straight into my heart: Buffy the Buff Orpington.

She was the flock's wild child—I'd requested one extra chick of a mystery breed from the hatchery—and a troublemaker from the start. Out of thirty chicks, she was the only one who suffered from persistent pasty butt. I cleaned her blonde bottom twice a day, taking her into the house for whichever torturous method seemed to be working best at the moment.

Each time, two-inch-tall Buffy complained so loudly that the cat ran away and hid.

After she conquered her pasty butt problem at one and a half weeks—when the chicks were just barely big enough to fly out of the brooder—Buffy became the mischief-maker who led an exodus every time I removed the lid. She endeared herself by not running away with her freedom, like some of the chickens, but by simply using it to watch whatever I was doing—sometimes scooting up my arm for a better view.

Oh, and there's one more thing that the poultry books don't tell you: it only takes a few hours for the sweet, personable little chicks you've fallen in love with to turn into bloodthirsty cannibals.

. . . .

At first, there was just one victim. One victim, with fourteen potential perpetrators. There wasn't any obvious evidence that would aid in charging a certain individual with the crime: no smoking gun, no bloody beak. Just one Ameraucana with a large open wound at the base of her tail, and fourteen other chicks going about their business as usual, as though they had no idea what caused the damage.

I removed the wounded Ameraucana from the first brooder—the chicks had been split into two tubs, fifteen in each—applied antibacterial ointment to her wound, and placed her in a separate container with one other chick for company. A hospital room, so to speak, with the amiable and undersized Runt for a nurse.

Then I turned back to my fourteen possible criminals. Whodunit? Was it the Red Rooster by the feeding trough with a beak? The White Leghorn by the waterer with a claw? I squatted over the brooder to see if I could pick out any aggressors. No one bit.

I called a longtime poultry-owning friend, hoping for an empathic response. Instead he displayed a disconcerting level of surprise. "You have chicks eating each other? I've had full-grown hens do that, but never chicks."

Clearly, my ravenous girls needed to move out to the coop, and pronto. In the meantime, I divided them up into six different boxes, hoping that less crowding would result in less eating each other. Three birds in the cat carrier, twelve split among three different cardboard boxes, and the remaining fifteen split between the original two brooders.

This meant six waterers, six feeders, and six litters to monitor. And, just to make sure they had enough fresh air, each morning I ferried all six containers out from the garage to the backyard, and then back into the garage each night. Tending these rambunctious teenagers had become a full-time job: it was time they left the nest.

In the midst of sowing, watering, weeding, and farmers' marketing, Emmett and I also started working double time on the coop, screwing together salvaged wood scraps, stapling wire mesh, and bolting down metal roofing. All the while, we tried to keep the structure small enough to move in a pick-up truck, should the time come when we need to cart our chickens off to another piece of land. Our challenge was to give the chickens adequate space—at least two interior square feet per bird, in addition to a huge yard—while also keeping their home portable. After scribbling dozens of floor plans onto brown paper napkins, we accomplished our goal by making a stackable, two-story coop whose component pieces could come apart for easy transport. We included a foot-long chicken wire skirt on the bottom level to discourage predators from digging past the walls.

By the time the new home was ready to go, three more chicks had been cannibalized. The four patients—plus nurse Runt—stayed back in the garage-turned-infirmary, while we shuttled the other twenty-five off to the coop.

We spent the better part of the first day trying to teach the birds how to use the ramp that connected the coop's two stories. Their food was on the upper floor, their water on the lower, so they'd either use the ramp or quickly become hungry or thirsty. When we tucked them in for the night, Buffy was leading the charge with a handful of chicks who'd become ramp-savvy.

The following morning, I drove over to the field to check on my babies. I was relieved to hear cheeping as I approached the coop—they'd made it through their coldest night yet. As we checked on them throughout the day, more and more chicks were learning to navigate the ramp. At dusk, they hunkered down for another chilly night.

Only four chicks had decided to sleep on the upper level, right up against the screen door: Buffy, a White Leghorn, and two Ameraucanas. "Should we move them down? They'll be warmer that way." Emmett nodded, and we tucked the chicks in with the rest of the flock downstairs.

It was the last time we would see them. In the morning, Emmett's father drove over to town to tell us they were gone.

. . . .

I was just finishing up breakfast. Before I had a clue what was happening, Emmett was walking toward me with his hands extended, sobbing.

"I'm sorry, I'm so sorry," he sputtered. He reached for my shoulders; I pushed him away.

"No!" I shouted. "What happened?"

"They're gone," he said. "They're all gone. My dad went to the coop this morning, and they're all gone."

"No," I told him. "Let's go. We have to go find them."

Emmett drove me over to the field; my head was in my hands and I couldn't stop saying no. But when we pulled up to the coop, no Buffy rushed to the screen door to say hello. No cheeps greeted our arrival—just the silence left behind by twenty-five young birds.

It took only moments to piece together the night's events. Despite the wire skirt, a fox had dug a hole, one foot in diameter, clear under the coop—a hole that terminated precisely where the chicks had snuggled down to sleep. Precisely where I'd tucked four birds in with the rest of the flock last night.

I tried once more to say no but the word became too heavy, sinking before it left my mouth, finally falling out as a wet rage of unfiltered noise. My vision blurred. It took me a few minutes to find a voice.

"I hate this place," I said. "I never want to live here. The one thing I try to do to make myself a home, and it goes to shit. It's ruined. Fuck this place. I fucking hate it."

Emmett tried to gather me in his arms but I shoved him off. I threw a rock at the unrepentant hillside, took off my shoes, threw those, screamed a few times, threw another rock. Then, stiff with the anger that was keeping my guilt at bay, I walked around the coop to survey the damage. Emmett quietly collected my shoes.

The fox hadn't felt compelled to take all of the birds he killed. He abandoned two bodies and a wing by the inconvenient salad bed. Inside the coop's lower level, one White

Leghorn lay half-buried in the loosened soil, her yellow legs jutting out at an awkward angle, her white wings gray with dirt. No obvious marks on her—but all around the coop floor, dark spatters of blood and clumps of feathers.

While behind me Emmett walked up the hill, calling, "Here, chick-chick-chick" to see if there were any survivors, I moved the ramp to look for more bodies.

Cheep, cheep.

I froze. I must be imagining things. I glanced down at the Leghorn: still very dead. The wooden ramp was in my hands and I pulled it up the rest of the way onto the second floor of the coop. The chickens wouldn't need it anymore.

Cheep, cheep.

There, where the ramp had been, was a bird: one survivor out of twenty-five.

It was the chick I'd named Penguin after her fluffy, gray baby down. In the instant that I saw her there—admittedly out of an entirely maudlin sense of metaphor—I renamed her Hope, thinking that the following couple of days would tell whether she'd live or die.

In my quick assessment of the situation, her odds didn't look good. First of all, she'd always been one of the flightiest chicks. She never wanted to be held and always avoided human contact at all costs, but now she was hurt enough not to try running away. I grabbed some food from the top floor and extended my hand. She lurched toward me, each movement off-balance, her right wing sagging. Blood stained her neck feathers. Five puncture wounds peppered her back and chest. Clearly, she'd been in the jaws of death, had somehow managed to get away, and had hidden by herself in the darkest, tightest corner of the coop through a long and cold night.

Emmett didn't find any more chicks, and he came back down to the coop to help me pull the White Leghorn out of the dirt. I couldn't quite bring myself to do it, so he picked her up by one yellow leg, gingerly. When I saw her dangling, I reached out and placed a hand underneath her cold torso, cradling her the way I would have when she was alive.

Surely we'd find most of them soon—maybe roosting high in a nearby tree, or snuggled down in an old abandoned shed, somewhere together. Twenty-four birds just couldn't be gone. But on the car ride home, my body resigned itself to what my mind couldn't: tears kept creeping down my face, even as my one little wounded thing with feathers snuggled in the crook of my neck, burying her head in my hair, cheeping.

. . . .

To be perfectly honest, I wanted to give up. I wanted to buy a one-way plane ticket to somewhere I didn't know anyone, so I could revel in my failure and wallow in my misery without fear of retribution. I didn't want to face customers at the farmers' market, who had been hearing all of the adorable details of my chicken project; I didn't want to confess to family and friends that I had failed to protect twenty-five of the tiny creatures under my care. To hell with livestock. I couldn't care that much about things that died so easily—it was simpler not to eat eggs.

And at the same time, I was furious with myself for not knowing better. In middle school I'd read *A Day No Pigs Would Die*. Spoiler alert: the goddamn pig dies! And that's *after* the dog is mortally wounded. You're not supposed to name things, you're not supposed to anthropomorphize them, and you're sure as hell not supposed to love them. Livestock is inevitably killed, and the fool with the heart just ends up hurt.

Why bother? Why do this at all? Emmett and I could pretend that my little tirade was just brief, grief-stricken insanity, but the real question remained: what was I doing here, and would it ever start to feel like home? The things I cared about most didn't seem to work. I was constantly reminded of my foreignness, whether it was the interactions with people I didn't know at the farmers' market who had known Emmett since he was knee-high, or the fact that I could never remember the names of the twenty or so tiny towns that are sprinkled across the county, let alone have any clue how to get to one of them. I was always nodding dumbly and pretending I knew what someone was talking about; it was like I didn't speak the language.

And then there was the sheer awkwardness of explaining my relationship to the land and to the farm, a relationship I didn't even understand myself. I was some sort of sharecropper, I supposed, tangentially related by an entirely undefined relationship. The people who owned the land were not my in-laws, not even my almost in-laws; they were my boyfriend's parents. I had moved here, but at what point would I become family? At what point would I become a part of the land, and at what point would it become a part of me?

Even my tantrum—the very act of throwing my shoes— reminded me that I was an alien. My feet were used to sea-smoothed stones and sand, not this prickly oak meadow full of thorns and burrs. This wasn't a place to walk barefoot. When Emmett gathered my shoes I wanted to throw them again, but my feet thought better of it. As soon as he wasn't paying attention I slipped them back on, feeling rather self-conscious, and entertained fleeting visions of getting in the car and driving to the coast. There was a time, early in our relationship, that whenever I was upset or feeling lost I would disappear to do just that. It scared Emmett because he knew I drove fast, windows down, heat and music blasting, sometimes taking long-exposure photos as I passed the semis on Route 1 late at night. So I stopped. I'd given up the wandering, but where was the safety and comfort I thought I'd get in return? I once promised myself that I would sail around the world. Maybe it was finally the time to do that—cut and run until Emmett wore out his farming fantasies and we could settle down somewhere neutral.

But there were still six chickens. Six chickens that, by the simple act of purchasing them, I had promised to care for. To quit now was to lose my credibility as a farmer, and for some reason that mattered. In the face of failed crops, farmers replant. Thrown from a horse, they remount. Faced with crashing produce prices, they expand. It may be nonsensical from an intellectual's point of view, but to do otherwise would be to admit defeat. And defeat was unacceptable.

Besides, Emmett, the one who didn't want chickens in the first place, was suddenly telling me to get more chickens. I think that mostly he wanted to do anything to pull me out of my guilty wallowing, but still, the fact that he had suddenly become a chicken advocate was a shock to my system. We'll fix the coop, he told me. Put a wooden floor on it, make sure the new chicks are safe. You don't even have to work on it, I'll take care of it. We can't know everything—but we can keep trying.

So, like those stubborn old men who continue to pour money into failing enterprises—thinking that maybe just a bigger, better, shinier tractor would do the trick—I agreed to buy more chicks. In fact, rather than just replacing the lost twenty-four birds, I ordered twenty-eight, bringing the

grand chicken total to thirty-four.* And instead of just buy-
ing the standard White Leghorns, Rhode Island Reds, and
Ameraucanas, I ordered another Buff Orpington. And a
Silver-Laced Wyandotte. And a Barred Rock. Take that, Fox.

Five hours after I plucked Hope out of her bloody, broken
coop, I dialed the hatchery's phone number. Just my luck, they
happened to have all of the breeds I wanted in stock today.
Would I like them shipped out this afternoon?

Feeling just a wee bit emotional, I said yes. And the following morning, one month to the day after I picked up my
first group of babies, I got my second call from the post office.

We picked up the box, brought it home, settled the new
chicks into the brooder. Quickly, this time, quietly. Practiced.
And then we drove back to the field for the funeral.

We buried three bodies and one wing. The bodies were
unnamed: two Rhode Island Reds, one White Leghorn. The
wing was Buffy's. Emmett marked the graves with pieces of
abalone shell, and I placed rosebuds in their hollows: two reds,
one white, one yellow.

It was then that I understood what poultry owners meant
when they said that chickens didn't take up much of your
time—unless something went wrong. The four-bird funeral
didn't mark the end of the dying. Instead, it seemed to kick-
start a streak of tragedies. It didn't rain but it poured.

The following day I went into the garage to check on the
new chicks and found one tiny White Leghorn mysteriously
dead inside the brooder. As I crouched beside the glowing
plastic crate, the hairs along my neck rose and my chest tight-
ened. I squeezed my eyes shut. When I opened them, the little

---

*Impossibly, a neighbor found a second survivor the following afternoon—a Rhode Island
Red, christened L.C. or Lucky Chicken, who wandered outside for twenty-four hours
before being found several hundred yards from the coop.*

yellow body was still there, deflated and flat, eyelids closed, legs bent, and toes curled inward.

Worried that somehow it might be getting too cold in the garage—that she might have been smothered in a pile-up, despite the heat lamp—I moved the brooder into the house. During the following morning's routine check-in, I discovered a Rhode Island Red with a broken leg, barely able to hobble. I moved her into a tissue box inside the brooder to protect her from her overzealous sisters, checked on her constantly, splinted her broken leg with a toothpick, and adjusted the angle of the heat lamp to make sure she was warm, but not too warm. Splitting my caretaking time between her and Hope— who was receiving antibiotics, a microwaved heat pad, and brief social visits with the cannibalized sisters that had been kept back—I coaxed the tiny Rhode Island girl along for days, forcing her to eat and drink, waking twice a night to try and get food into her every few hours. But her appetite was weak. After a week, she hadn't grown one bit. The other chicks were twice her size. She passed away in the night after one of my check-ins; Emmett found her in the morning. Another funeral.

The day after she died, I peered into the brooder and found the rooster—by far the biggest chick of the lot, a fat jolly fellow I'd dubbed Santa—unable to walk. His toes were curled up into balls, and he was half-shuffling his way over to the food trough.

Since I'd spent the past week nursing two sick chicks, I hadn't taken the time to hold each bird each day, like I had with the first bunch. So the second flock was flightier. When I opened the brooder lid all of the chicks spooked; the fat little rooster was bowled over onto his side by the onslaught. My heart broke just a little more and I scooped him up. At least I already had a hospital container ready.

Have you ever gotten one of those fortunes that tell you too little, too late? At a rare dinner out, I was informed by a shattered cookie: For better luck, wait until spring.

Fighting fate, I turned to BackyardChickens.com and found a possible solution: boots. While some farmers recommended culling chicks like Santa—the trait is most likely due to a vitamin deficiency in the mother hen, but could possibly be genetic—I was willing to do whatever it took to keep this boy alive. Up to and including fashioning chick boots out of cardboard and taping them onto the feet of the rooster in an attempt to straighten out his wayward toes.

Like it or not, this tubby little rooster was teaching me something about my relationship with my flock. While he may have been just the next thing in a long line of problems, the challenge reminded me of one of the reasons why I was raising birds in the first place: to give them a good home and a nurturing protector. And if I was a lousy protector, I was going to be make up for it by being one hell of a nurturer.

The average American chicken sorely needs a better life. More than 8 billion chickens are born each year[26] into unnatural, degrading conditions. About 300 million of them lay eggs, while 8 billion others are bred for meat.[27] Layer or fryer, they share in common a brutal reality: overcrowding, no access to the outdoors, de-beaking to avoid cannibalism, and remorseless culling of the weak. We have come to call this modern industrial agriculture. Before the 1950s, though, the poultry business was dominated by a different way of thinking: animal husbandry.

According to author and animal scientist Bernard Rollin, "In husbandry, we put animals into the environment best suited for them to survive and thrive . . . and then augment their natural ability to function with provisions of food during famine, water during drought, help in birthing, protection from predators, medical attention, and so on."[28] The traditional ethic of animal husbandry revolves around an unwritten contract between a farmer and his or her animals. A good husband(wo)man will care for the animals when they fall ill—or get curly toes—even if it is not economically profitable to do so. Rollin witnessed this attitude among Colorado ranchers who were experiencing an abnormally high number of calves being afflicted with scours, which is livestock-speak for diarrhea. "Every rancher I met had spent more money on treating the disease than was economically justified by the calves' market value," Rollin recounts. "When I asked these men why they were being 'economically irrational,' they were adamant in their responses: 'It's part of my bargain with the animal.'"

In contrast, industrial agriculture places profit, productivity, and efficiency above animal welfare. If an animal is sick, it's generally more economical to kill the animal than to expend resources nurturing it back to health. The average dairy, for instance, knocks off over 30 percent of its herd *each year*.[29] If a cow's milk production drops, or she contracts mastitis, a disease, or a physical injury, her time is up. This practice makes animals into little more than raw materials or production units—as opposed to the living, feeling creatures I saw darting across my brooder each time I lowered a handful of fresh feed.

In a confinement poultry operation, Santa probably would have been immediately killed,* not given a chance at survival. In my operation, he was taking a little extra care and attention, but with a bit of luck he'd be on his feet again soon. The

---

*Santa also probably would have been killed simply because he was a male chick, making him much less valuable than egg-laying hens. The culling of rooster chicks is common industry practice in commercial egg operations—and also hatcheries, such as the one from which I purchased my chicks.

opportunity to treat chickens with respect and care—to practice good animal husbandry—is part of why I ordered these chicks in the first place. I wouldn't eat factory-raised eggs, but I hadn't given up on eggs altogether. By taking the responsibility into my own hands, I could ensure that the eggs I ate—and the eggs that my customers ate—were raised according to the principle of animal husbandry, which dates back all the way to the biblical tenet that "the good shepherd giveth his life for the sheep" (or in this case, the chicken owner giveth all her waking hours for her chickens).

If I happened to be in a positive mood—which, quite frankly, was less often than not—I could convince myself that my series of disasters up to and including Santa's curly toes were just nature's way of reminding me of my bargain with the animals. I was their caretaker.

For four days, I carried the baby rooster around in a small plastic box with me everywhere I went. The afternoons were sunny and warm; while I weeded the salad bed, he stayed in his box in the car. Three or four times an hour, his shrieks rang out through the cracked windows and across the open field. The sound let me know that he'd managed to get his clunky cardboard boots stuck behind him again—that he was lying rather pathetically on his fat belly, head tilted back to screech. I would go over, set him straight, and resume weeding. On the fourth day, after I'd already righted Santa a number of times, he started screeching again. This time, as I peered through the car window, I could see that he'd managed to hobble through his small water dish, soaking both of his boots.

Since nothing was wrong from his perspective—by the time I got over to the car, he was quietly sitting on his damp haunches, head down in his jar lid of food—I could only assume that he was gloating over the fact that I had to cut a fifth pair of chick boots from my rapidly diminishing cereal box.

On day five of boot camp, my toil was rewarded: I removed the offensive footwear and Santa walked. To celebrate, I went down to the feed store and picked up two more chicks to replace the two I had lost. This time, I chose a Light Brahma—a little black and yellow fluff-ball with feathered feet—and another Silver Laced Wyandotte. Emmett expressed some consternation at my purchases; in turn, I accused him of killing my joy. Feeling that I might have spoken too harshly, I named the Light Brahma Joy, and told Emmett she'd be his chicken. Besides, I pointed out, the two new girls would keep Santa company until he was steady enough on his newly flat feet to handle all twenty-seven ladies.

. . . .

It was nighttime and a full moon illuminated the hill behind the chicken yard. Some days it wasn't so bad, this inland thing; the wind could almost be an ocean breeze, the undulating grassland the Pacific. We walked up the hill, laughing at the clarity of our moon shadows, the way they stretched out like atavistic giants, wobbling drunk over depressions before disappearing into the darkness of an oak tree.

Three foxes materialized. At first I thought I must be imagining them, figment dolphins leaping in and out of a prairie sea. But Emmett saw them too: a mother, it looked like, with two kits weaving behind her.

City Lynda would have cooed over these foxes, the striking setting, the wild moment. But at that moment, I was torn between reciting Wordsworth and throwing rocks. Thinking of the chickens, Country Lynda picked up a rock. I wasn't raised to think of foxes and raccoons as enemies; I wasn't groomed to be a farmer. I went to grad school, scribbled poetry in the margins of notebooks while listening to lectures on biology and ecology. But as much as I was an environmentalist—one who fully understood the value of apex predators in an ecosystem—I was also a farmer and livestock keeper. One who had a little bit of trouble letting go of that rock.

But I *did* drop it. And with Santa healthy—in fact, handily beating the entire flock to the feed dish—it was in the realm of possibility that things would be okay. I still teared up thinking about the lost birds, and my caretaking involved an unprecedented level of paranoia. But the new flock grew on me. They earned names. The Silver Laced Wyandotte with the stripes running down her back became Skunk. The slightly slow, bottom-of-the-pecking-order Ameraucana who liked to burrow under the other chicks became Dozer. The white chicken with blue feet was Booby. The Barred Rock, with her black bodysuit and white dot on her chest, was Tux—and she, not the new Buff Orpington, would carry on the spirit of Buffy, the first to fly out of the brooder just to see what was going on in the greater world. Later, she'd be the first to greet me at the coop and fly to my shoulder or stand on my foot, waiting to be picked up. There was our surprise Mo, too—a White Leghorn "she" that turned out to be a "he," with a huge floppy comb (a Mohawk) and pendulous jowls far too big for his body. He became a chivalrous rooster, always hunting down tasty treats for the ladies or performing a courtship dance for them, flaring his white wings, head bobbing.

And, of course, there was always Hope.

Chapter 4:

SWEET SAMPLES

· ·

Heirloom Tomatoes

I was experiencing unfortunate flashbacks.

In high school, a particularly cruel physics teacher forced me to construct some sort of bottle rocket launch pad. Lost as to how to accomplish such a task, I screwed up the courage to venture into the local hardware store. Blonde, bitter, and apparently hell-bent on playing up the role of incompetent female, I wandered lost amid hundreds of different types of nuts, bolts, and other small, shiny metal objects. At some point I even started humming Disney tunes. The crappy ones from *Pocahontas*. I was eventually rescued by my pragmatic female science partner, who had managed to find whatever small, shiny things we needed, but the trauma remains.

Now I found myself in a different sort of hell. It was one with the temperature and humidity of a New Jersey summer, and approximately sixty different types of tomato starts, which were mysteriously mixed in with pepper starts and other small, bright green things. Different setting, same overwhelming feeling of failure.

I was in the greenhouse of a wholesale nursery sheepishly buying tomato plants because, well, we nuked ours. I was well aware that real farmers grew tomatoes from seed and only fuck-ups bought them in six-packs. When we explained to the owner of the nursery that we were farmers, he was confused and figured we were buying the starts to resell at market. We had to explain that we were planning on selling the fruit, not the plants (in a couple of months, assuming we didn't kill the plants first). And while no self-respecting farmer would purchase tomato starts, no self-respecting farm stand would be without heirloom tomatoes—that farmers' market icon, that sure sign of summer, that nonspherical, nonconformist, tie-dyed, sweet and succulent fruit.

That one we *didn't* grow from seed. My ego was bruised and Emmett, cooing over tomato starts, wasn't helping it.

"Whoa," he said, and pointed out a six-pack of Black Plums. "This tag says 7/11. Does that mean it was planted two weeks ago? The thing has to be six inches tall."

Our second attempt at tomato seedlings, planted a month before, had grown to only three quarters of an inch tall and only a few of them had managed to don a second set of leaves.

I tried to shrug it off. "They probably jack them up with chemical fertilizers."

While my catty comment may have been true, it didn't negate the fact that the ability to grow tomatoes from seed was a skill. And the one thing that could replace acquired skill (besides lady luck, who had thus far spurned us) was technology. This nursery had both: it was a family operation that has been churning out seedlings for years. And the voluminous greenhouse possessed an automatic ventilation system and an automatic watering system, which meant that the temperature and moisture content of the soil were regulated without human intervention. Even the size of the greenhouse was to its advantage: that much moist air, with the ventilation windows shut, could maintain a constant temperature through the cool nights.

We were a bit more manual. Our advanced technology (typically preceded by, "Shit! The tomatoes!") entailed frantically racing up the hill to yank the plastic cover off the hoophouse on a hot day, grabbing the hose, and guessing at the spray setting and length of time required to satiate the seedlings without over-saturating the soil.

"Box Car Willie," Emmett murmured. "What a great name."

We rooted around the platforms filled with tomato starts. Box Car Willie snuggled in flats with Radiator Charlie's Mortgage Lifter, while Pruden's Purple and Stupice bedded down on another table. Black Plum, Sun Gold, Striped German, Cherokee Purple, Sungella: we were new to the tomato world and could only guess at what sorts of fruits those mysterious names would generate. I put my money on the more creative monikers—the Box Car Willies, Striped Germans, and Radiator Charlie's Mortgage Lifters of the world. But more important than literary sensibility was size. We were hunting for the smallest, youngest starts. We didn't want supermodels; we wanted toads. A leggy two-foot-tall tomato plant stretching out of a tiny plastic pot was distinctly inferior to a short, stocky plant. And if a seedling already had flowers, forget it. Fresh starts were best. They'd be most likely to take the transition of transplanting smoothly, and squat stalks were more able to bear the weight of mature fruit than long, thin vines.

We picked out eighty plants. As we forked over eighty-nine dollars and pulled the car up to the greenhouse to load up the little green things, we felt a bit silly but excited at the thought of what was to come. We thought of the heavy, brilliantly colored fruit tucked in their rainforest of leafy vines. It was going to be one hell of a harvest.

....

Unfortunately, I enjoy the concept of tomatoes far more than the actual fruit. You simply couldn't ask for a more sensual piece of produce. Round, ripe, firm yet yielding—squeezing a tomato is about as close to squeezing human flesh as one can get. (For all the jokes made about melons, they're hard and unfriendly, nothing like the real thing.) And consider the color: while melons hide their brilliance inside dull rinds, tomatoes let it all hang out, lustrous and naked.

But while I'm drawn in by their soft skin and vibrant blushes, I confess that my love affair with tomatoes runs only skin deep. Because I was raised primarily on meat and carbohydrates, the texture—in particular the sliminess surrounding the seed pockets—is a deal breaker.

I can't deny, though, that the flavor of the tomato is excellent. To enjoy the balance of sweetness and acidity without the troublesome texture, I used to partake of sauce and ketchup only. (Don't scoff: According to the USDA under Reagan, ketchup is, in fact, a fruit.) My gateway dish was the lightly broiled tomato, halved and topped with parmesan and bread crumbs; from there, I got hooked on totally raw bruschetta (with plenty of garlic, basil, and balsamic) and eased my way slowly into salted sliced tomatoes (balsamic and a fork mandatory). I still can't bite into one like an apple—even the sweetest whole cherry tomatoes are difficult for me to pop in my mouth. But as shrimp and lobster literally induce my gag reflex, I readily admit that my palate is handicapped.

In all fairness to the tomato, my culinary caprice doesn't deserve any historical support. And yet a cautionary attitude toward the fruit does have precedent—plenty of precedent. In 1820, the legend goes, a man named Colonel Robert Gibbon Johnson made a brave announcement: at high noon on September 26 he would stand in front of the Boston courthouse and *eat an entire bushel of tomatoes*. People gathered outside the courthouse to watch the spectacle, awaiting the silly sop's imminent death. After all, this man was about to consume not one but twenty or so of the poisonous fruits. The townspeople were shocked—and, let's face it, gravely disappointed—when Colonel Johnson lived to tell the tale.

A family of five in Hawking County, Tennessee, wasn't so lucky. On an ordinary day in 1963, the Mason family* settled down for a midday dinner of split pea soup, pasta with meat sauce, and the season's first sliced tomato. According to firsthand accounts, minutes after three of the family members sampled the tomato, they found themselves staggering across the room—which had, oddly enough, begun to ebb and flow around them—hit by waves of nausea. The son drove them to the hospital. There, the father swatted imaginary swarms of insects while the mother battled violent, whole-body convulsions, and all three suffered dry mouth and dilated pupils—all from a single slice of a seemingly innocent fruit.[30]

Of course, the tomato's history didn't commence in 1820, and the legend of its toxicity goes back hundreds of years before Colonel Johnson allegedly rendered a not-guilty verdict with his compelling argument at the Boston courthouse. Like Paddington Bear, tomatoes originated in darkest Peru. Wild tomatoes—of which ten surviving species have been

---

Mason was not the real surname of the family, but rather the name used by the reporter who covered the story in the 1965 May edition of the New Yorker.

identified by botanists—populated the Andean highlands. Sporting small yellow flowers that matured into small yellow fruit, ancestral tomatoes bear little resemblance to today's multicolored behemoths.

From Peru the tomato apparently made its way—how, we don't entirely know—to Central America. There the Aztecs dubbed it *xitomatl* ("plump thing with a navel") and did something brilliant: they combined the proto-tomato with peppers and corn to make the world's first salsa, a culinary achievement not to be taken lightly.

From there, the saga of xitomatl is just too entertaining to pass up. Spanish explorers, in the process of annihilating Central American Aztecs, picked up a few xitomatl and brought them back to Europe. Some historians believe they came with Cortez after he took over Tenochtitlan (present day Mexico City) in 1521. Others point to Christopher Columbus for his obvious schoolchild cachet. But as is the case with most of our history, no one really knows how precisely it happened; we just know that tomatoes somehow made their way to Europe. More precisely, we know that the first documented record of the tomato was penned in 1544 by an Italian physician/botanist elegantly named Pietro Andrea Mattioli. You can almost hear the word "tomato" in his name, can't you? And yet Pietro Mattioli renamed the "plump thing with a navel" the "golden apple," or *pomi d'oro*. This later became simply *pomodoro*, the modern Italian word for tomato.

Although the name may sound like a shining endorsement, it also possesses undertones of Eden's dangerous fruit. Mattioli correctly classified the tomato as belonging to the nightshade family, and because other members of the nightshade family were known to induce hallucination and death when ingested, many folks were understandably skeptical about biting into the newfangled golden apple. Mind you, these same people were willing to drip nightshade poison into the sensitive mucous membranes of their own eyes. The tomato's close cousin, belladonna—literally translated as "pretty woman"—was so named because elegant ladies would squirt it in their eyes to induce pupil dilation (an act that belongs in encyclopedias next to foot binding and five-inch stilettos, under Things We Shouldn't Do to Our Bodies to Look Sexy).

Alas, the Italians got off to a rocky start with the fruit that would eventually become a focal point of their national cuisine. Meanwhile, the French found themselves romanced by the tomato's latent sensuality. Poison? *Non, mes amis, c'est la pomme d'amour.* Nightshade be damned: in France, the tomato became known as the love apple, an aphrodisiac that was especially palatable when paired with butter, cream, a hearty cheese, wine, and crusty bread—and for all that, it remained remarkably friendly to the figure.

Despite French passion for the fruit, the tomato's reputation continued to suffer. In the 1700s it was dealt a severe blow by Swedish scientist Carl Linnaeus. Nightshade hallucinations often involve a feeling of flying, so nightshade was popularly associated with witchcraft; in German folklore, witches used nightshade as a lure for werewolves. This history clearly factored into Linnaeus' scientific name for the tomato: *Solanum lycopersicum.* Leave it to a Northern European to take "plump thing with a navel"—also known as "golden/love apple"—and turn it into "quieting wolf-peach." Scottish botanist Philip Miller later upgraded the tomato to *Lycopersicon esculentum* or "edible wolf-peach."

Which brings us back to the question of poison. Why weren't the tomatoes consumed by the Mason family in 1963 edible? As it turned out, the family's green-thumb son had grafted a tomato vine onto jimson weed, a hardy, frost-tolerant close cousin of the tomato. On the surface, the idea was brilliant—and, in fact, it's the same concept that lies behind all commercial fruit production today. Take a delicious, but perhaps less-than-vigorous, fruiting plant and stick it onto the most vigorous root stock you can find. With a bit of luck, you'll end up with healthier plants, consistent production in a variety of environments, and more fruit.

The Masons' grafting experiment didn't go quite so smoothly. The graft took, and soon jimson tomatoes were flourishing in the Masons' backyard. But when the family sat down to taste their first slice of homegrown summer, they learned the hard way that not all plant varieties are suitable as rootstocks—and that, in fact, we're very lucky to be able to eat tomatoes at all.

The leaves of the tomato plant are toxic if ingested. However, unlike jimson weed, they do not produce toxins that are carried up to and concentrated within the fruit. (Word to the wise: If your goal is to produce a healthful, edible fruit, don't graft anything onto a plant that has a habit of concentrating poison in fruit.)

Today, Americans spend more than four billion dollars[31] on more than 160 varieties of perfectly edible golden apples. Thanks to intrepid tomato eaters like Colonel Johnson and Thomas Jefferson (who also reputedly ate a tomato in public to prove it wasn't poisonous), by the 1800s the tomato was not only accepted in America, it was turning into an industry. Seed catalogue sales soared. Farmers developed varieties suited to their regional growing conditions and tastes. The tomato became what it is today: a food fit for everyday sandwiches, soups, sauces, casseroles—pretty much anything, in fact, except dessert.

Would that the history of the tomato concluded there and xitomatl fruited happily ever after. But the tomato—sweet/succulent, toxic/healthful—continues its series of identity crises. In the United States, different legislative bodies have, at different times, declared the tomato to be a vegetable, a fruit, or both. In 1883 the Supreme Court determined it to be a vegetable. Yes, that's right: not only did the highest court in the land debate what food group the tomato belongs in, they also got it wrong. Despite the existence of botany and taxonomy, both well-developed disciplines in the late 1800s, the Court decided that the culinary uses of the tomato (for use with a main dish rather than a dessert) rendered it a vegetable for tariff purposes—a designation that continues to this day.

Meanwhile, botanists, biologists, and anyone who has passed a reasonably robust biology course would argue that a tomato is undeniably a fruit. It's not the round sensuality of the thing that renders it a fruit, but the actual act of flower sex. The male stamen fertilizes the female pistil—tomatoes are self-pollinating, so this process takes place entirely within a single flower, triggered by the vibration of a breeze or a bee's wings—and produces fertile seeds encased in a nutritious body that provides a dispersal mechanism for the seeds. In short, fruit. (Note that eggplants, cucumbers, and squash share this scientific definition despite vegetative culinary use, but no one cares enough about them to fight about it.)

And so we return to the tomato plant—fruit, vegetable, deadly, and delicious—and the process of growing it.

. . . .

In short order, we unloaded eighty seedlings from the station wagon and set them down on the field. They'd spend

Beets, beans, potatoes, and tomatoes: the farm was
starting to take shape.

two nights adjusting to life outside the comforts of the
greenhouse—"hardening off" in farmer-speak—before being
transplanted into two long rows.

We decided to prune the vines, another point of debate
in the tomato world. We'd trim off the runners, shoots that
sprout between forks in the vine, effectively channeling more
of the plant's energy into producing fruit rather than bushy
foliage. Is trimming runners worth the effort? Some farmers
say no, others yes. Pruned plants can tower overhead, tied up to
six- or even eight-foot wooden stakes, while unpruned plants
tend to be shorter and bushier. The answer to the pruning
debate often depends on scale. We decided to prune because
we had only eighty plants, all of which were indeterminate,
meaning they'd produce fruit continuously for the duration of
the season. (Determinate plants set fruit all at once, so there's
little sense in pruning them.) While most large-scale commercial tomato farms grow determinate tomatoes—allowing

harvesting machines to come through and essentially rip out the entire plant while pulling the fruit—we preferred plants that would keep on giving week after week.

Correction: We preferred plants that *should* keep on giving week after week.

After dutifully amending the soil, carefully transplanting the tomato starts, pruning all runners, and religiously watering the plants, you'd think the tomato plants might consent to setting fruit. Instead, several decided to protest, and showed their dissatisfaction by refusing to grow, allowing their leaves to curl and shrivel, or donning an odd spotted motif. When that happens, gardening books told us, the dutiful gardener must rip out the affected plants and burn them lest his whole field become contaminated. Oh, and we couldn't replant tomatoes in those fields for two to three years.

There's a reason large-scale commercial operations don't tend to grow heirloom tomatoes. Namely, heirloom tomatoes can be overly sensitive to insect-borne diseases like spotted wilt virus, mosaic virus, bacterial canker, septoria leaf spot, grey leaf spot, bacterial speck, bacterial spot, or syringae leaf spot. (They also crack open easily on the vine, and their irregular shapes and sizes make it tough to pack them efficiently by the tens of thousands.)

And unlike large-scale commercial operations, which harvest their tomatoes while they're still green and hard, ripening them through a complicated process using special hormone-triggering gasses, we'd wait to harvest our tomatoes until they were ready to eat. We'd be trucking them only five minutes down the road, after all. And vine-ripened fruit has a balanced blend of sugar and acid that is unparalleled: one reason why people shop at the farmers' market in the first place. Now, if only the vines would stay alive long enough to ripen the fruit.

Chapter 5:

LITTLE MONSTERS

··

Summer Squash

In a few short weeks, July had decidedly and undeniably turned the corner into August: the miracle month.

Scrawny seedlings had come into their own. No longer tentative, sprawling squash plants, bushy tomatoes, and bean hedges debuted with confidence, crowding out the weeds with their bright green gowns. Paparazzi bees swarmed the orange squash blossoms. The Patch was no longer a swath of dirt stitched with occasional green thread; it had become a bolt of rich green fabric ribbed by narrow dirt paths. We were over an acre now, which definitely pushed us past the garden category. At some point we blinked, and in that split second the farm assumed an air of ramshackle legitimacy. Small, none of the rows precisely straight, but prolific. Our series of screw-ups—dead seedlings, insect massacres, chicken funerals—was a distant dream. I wished it had been more gradual, that I could have built up slowly to the climax. But the transition was sudden. One day we were fretting over the loss of a squash plant that fell victim to a gopher;

the next, we were fielding a deluge. Hope and aspiration were replaced by the physical reality of constant harvest.

So this was what it felt like to be a farmer.

The night was warm. My knuckles itched. My forearms, ankles, calves, and shins itched. My palms itched—not that it meant, as legend dictates, that I'd be coming into money anytime soon. (Summer squash—the root of this itch—fetches two dollars per pound at most.)

As far as I could tell, to feel like a farmer was to feel consistently uncomfortable. And to look like a farmer at locations other than the farmers' market made other people uncomfortable, too. Overalls and a straw hat do not a farmer make: squash rash, cracked knuckles, and stained hands do.

Over the course of the season, different crops had modified my body. My skin revealed the most visible changes. The contact dermatitis that appeared like clockwork on Tuesdays and Fridays—harvest days—was courtesy of our squash plants. I couldn't bring myself to don long sleeves and pants in 100-degree weather, so I suffered the consequences of exposing my body's largest organ to the ravenous *Cucurbita pepo*. Tender squash fruits grow at the heart of the plant, sometimes several feet inside the monster's outermost reaches. These beasts belong in Jurassic Park: deep, fern-green foliage; long, thick stalks; massive leaves bigger than my head. And all of it festooned with tiny, sharp-toothed thorns—thorns that never quite puncture the skin, but irritate it enough to leave the unhappy harvester itching and scratching as she lies in bed at night, waiting for sleep to come. So my arms and legs were always a little red and chafed. The squash rash lasted about a day, and the late-night rake marks from my fingernails lasted the next two, until it was time to harvest squash again.

Then there were my hands, which would make a manicurist weep. I was proud of my shovel-ready palms, thickly callused in all the right places. I could, however, have done without the cracked fingertips and knuckles, and the splinters that were always appearing and disappearing and trading places with the inevitable abrasions and cuts.

I couldn't pin the cracks on any one plant—it was just a general weathering, exposure to the wind and sun and earth, that dried out my fingers and left them canyoned. But for the stains that reached from my fingertips to my palms, I could thank our earliest nightshades, the cherry tomatoes. If you've ever picked a few tomatoes off the vine, you might have noticed that your fingertips developed a slight green-brown tinge to them. If you pick a few hundred, that tinge turns into an inky brown encasement that stubbornly resists rinsing. With a lot of soap and scrubbing, you can dilute the stuff sufficiently to send some of it swirling down the drain. It is difficult enough to remove the substance from smooth skin, but I found that getting it out of the cracks was impossible.

Which is why my hands drew reactions at the grocery check stand: each imperfection was inked, the rough nails and split skin and abrasions and splinter-holes clearly outlined by the tomatoes' brown stains. When I placed my cereal boxes on the conveyor belt, those in line behind me must have wondered why hand soap, scrub brushes, and lotion weren't heaped in my shopping cart. But I had stopped striving for manicured hands. Mine were a work of art in their own right, a map of hard work and harvest.

The rest of my body was changing, too. I couldn't run a marathon or swim a mile. I couldn't remember the last time I exercised for the sake of exercising. Moving muscles for their own sake seemed silly when there were other things they should be doing, like weeding beets. There were always beets to weed. But the work-exercise was imperfect, unbalanced, turning me prematurely into an old fart. My breaking back, my sore neck, my stiff knees!

And always, my body was slightly warm with exhaustion, so bone-tired when it hit the bed that sleep should have been easy, if it weren't for the hot night and the ache in the back and the itching and Emmett tossing and turning beside me, making it hard to settle down and find that perfect place where everything could just sink toward the floor and stop work at last.

. . . .

NPR was on the radio, a comforting drone. As with so many market mornings, I wasn't sure exactly when I'd fallen asleep, nor was I entirely clear on why I was here in the passenger seat, pulling on socks as we drove down the dirt road to the field before the full moon had set. Emmett was just starting to pull the truck onto the shoulder that separated the road from the tomato rows when he slammed on the brake. My head, which had been leaning against the window, banged against the overhead handle.

"What the hell?"

The truck stopped and I swung open my door to the sound of a rushing river. In the glow of the headlights, I could see an island surrounded by muddy water. Beyond the island, a small sea lapped at the edges of the tomatoes, cucumbers, and summer squash. On the island perched a plastic chair, and to the plastic chair was taped a hand-written note.

My mind was as muddy as the water, and as the water sought the lowest point, so did my thoughts. We had left this place less than twelve hours ago, and what the fuck?

What the fuck.

Seriously, what the fuck?

The note was difficult to read, given the lack of light and our inability to get within ten feet of it. This was the middle of summer, which typically meant four months without rain, so we didn't exactly bring waders. Eventually I was able to recognize enough of the letters that I could fill in the ones I couldn't read like a crossword puzzle. The note, in Emmett's dad's handwriting, said something about sorry for backing into the pipe, it was late and dark, and that he'd be back in the morning to fix it.

Ah yes, the pipe. It clearly needed fixing, seeing as how it was cracked in half and gushing water like a ruptured fire hydrant, threatening to drown our newly productive summer crops.

"Well, it probably wasn't surrounded by water when he left the note there," I said slowly, trying to untangle the strange scene before me. Blinking repeatedly seemed to help. "That wouldn't make sense. He wouldn't wade out into the water to leave a note, right?"

Emmett walked along the mud-water shore before digging his cell phone out of his pocket and making the call.

"It's still going?" I heard a groan emanate from the cell phone; it matched my mood. "I shut off the main water valve last night. It should have stopped."

This is what it feels like to be a farmer: it feels like things are always going wrong, and that if only Equipment X wouldn't leak/break/rust/rupture/spontaneously discombobulate, life would be so much easier and the farm so much more productive.

The phone conversation droned on. I blew on my fingers, which had gotten cold, and watched the water rush out of the broken pipe. I found it sort of soothing, like watching a fire dance.

I heard a snap: Emmett closing his phone. "My dad's going to try and figure out why it didn't stop, and then try and fix it," Emmett said. We both eyed the geyser and the rising miniature lake that was a foot away from our precious Armenian cucumbers. "Hopefully it won't take too long."

Emmett headed to the back of the truck to pull out the harvest bins. For now we'd just circumnavigate Foggy River Lake to reach the vegetables. Flood or no, it was Saturday morning: time to harvest and hurry to the Healdsburg farmers' market.

. . . .

August summer mornings at the market were so bright they were almost cartoonlike. The squash, more than anything, was to blame: the Martha Stewart palette of daffodil yellows and lime greens seemed more suited to paint swatches than produce. I admit, Emmett and I had become a bit obsessed over the display aspect of the market. The farmers' market adage—pile 'em high and watch 'em fly—had given way to a more cultured approach. Pile them high in artfully arranged piles, the location of which were determined based on shade requirements, color, shape, and texture (in that order); accent as needed with baskets, tablecloths, and simple handwritten price signs; rearrange at least twice until perfect; then, watch them fly.

The rat's nest of crookneck squash, butter-yellow necks twined together, roiled next to a pile of staid, dark green Romanesco zucchini stacked neatly in rows. On the other side of the Romanesco, yellow zucchini, also neat. Next to them lay the twisty, pale green Armenian cucumbers. And then the patty pans lineup: acorn-shaped or scalloped-edged, clad in lime green and evergreen and daffodil yellow. The display was all about carefully controlled chaos and a feeling of exciting, but not messy, abundance. And of course, quality counted—everything here was harvested multiple times a week to keep it pretty and petite. We weren't selling summer squash monsters, the sort that families use as car bodies in the annual farmers' market zucchini car races. We were selling young, tender squashlets—as popular parlance has it, baby squash. And like all baby foods (lettuce, arugula, bok choy, cucumbers, beets) they were highly sought after by the foodie crowd.

The public's penchant for all things baby explained my rough hands and aching back: harvesting these days was constant. (And whenever we weren't harvesting, we were weeding or sowing new crops.) And we were just a small-scale farm—some would even nitpick that label and dub us market gardeners. We weren't Stetson-style ranchers with five thousand head of dusty Angus cattle destined for Fourth of July barbecues. Surveying our pretty-in-pastels display, one might fairly ask, why did my back hurt so much for something so *frou-frou?* And just who was I growing this pretty food for, anyway?

Definitely not for myself. I mean, we hadn't purchased produce from the grocery store in months, but Emmett and I weren't eating the picture-perfect market items. We ate what didn't make it to the display table: scarred zucchini, sunburned tomatoes and peppers, split cucumbers. Or we ate the deflated leftovers from the once-glorious piles at the end of the day. None of this produce, being classified as "seconds," could be sold at a grocery store, but it certainly tasted better than the majority of what grocery stores carry.

So who does eat the best of what Foggy River Farm grows? Many of the customers who enjoy our produce are of the holier–than–Whole Foods variety. It's too easy to satirize them: well-dressed and well-spoken; perhaps possessed of a small, fluffy white dog. The female of the couple has just concluded her morning yoga class and the male is trying to use his latest smart-phone application to see if our baby bok choy fits into his macrobiotic diet. But it's easy to satirize us, too: the hippie twenty-somethings just out of college, trying to become "real" people by eschewing the intellectual and giving manual labor a go. The caricatures don't mean much until you stick them together—at which point, one might wonder, what are the idealist hippie back-to-the-landers doing to save the world if they're only selling pretty patty pans to the wealthy eco-literati?

It's a good question.

"What are all of these called? And what's your favorite kind?" a young mother asked me as she leaned over the squash display, toddler in tow.

Emmett had momentarily disappeared, and I found myself scrambling to weigh zucchini, replenish the chard supply, and scoop handfuls of cherry tomatoes into cups.

"I like the Romanesco; it's an old Italian variety." She peered at the squash, clearly not helped. "That green ribbed one," I added, and jerked my head in the right direction. I was bent over, my head barely protruding above the display table, my hand deep in a box of Sun Golds.

"Do you have more?" a second, middle-aged woman asked, waving the last bunch of chard in my face.

"Yes, one second, I'm just helping another customer."

Market customers couldn't get enough of our sweet Sun Gold cherry tomatoes.

I finished scooping cherry tomatoes, poured two cups' worth into a plastic bag, handed them to an older gentleman, and went to weigh his bag of zucchini. Chard woman looked irritated; I had a fleeting vision of shoving her into Foggy River Lake.

The older man got my last two quarters, so in the midst of bunching more chard, I sold the young mother $3.75 of summer squash for $3.

As I snapped the rubber band around the chard bouquet, the woman eyed it warily. "I don't like the red kind, can you just give me yellow and white?"

"Good news," Emmett said, emerging from the cab of the truck. "My dad was able to shut off the water. Apparently the water system was somehow connected to our neighbor's house, which is why it kept going when he turned off the valve in the vineyard. When the neighbor called Dad and said he didn't have any water pressure, he figured it out. He's going to go get a new valve and pipe right now, so we should have water by the time we're done with the market."

Although it might have seemed that too much water was our current problem—and it very nearly was—it was also a problem to shut off all irrigation water. By the time we got back from the market, it would be 100 degrees F at the field, and our lettuces would be desperate for a drink.

"Anyway, it seems like the tomatoes closest to the flood might get a bit too much water, but other than that we should be fine. And it will probably just take longer for them to ripen, so it's not a big deal."

I was sorting through the chard bin for all the white- and yellow-stemmed leaves, and meanwhile chard woman had immersed herself in the zucchini display. She was picking out the tiniest squash she could find. She finally bought ten tiny squash for $2, plus a $1.50 bunch of chard (which she double-checked, hunting for any red leaves prior to purchase). But she gave me two quarters, so I forgave her.

Food is one of the few things on the planet that is both a pleasure and a necessity for the continuance of life. Sex is another, and perhaps housing. We don't enjoy the air we breathe according to how much we pay for it; we don't enjoy sex according to how much we pay for it, either, or at least most of us don't. But gustatory delight often comes with a price tag. That which is bland (American cheese) is cheap; that which is flavorful (Gruyère) costs more.

Of course, the distinctions don't always fall along flavor lines. Bland, chewy abalone runs sixty dollars per pound, while tender, flavorful chicken can be purchased for a fraction of that price. More to the point, at our market stand, you can buy tiny, two-inch summer squash that sport giant orange blossoms: fifty cents apiece. Or, you could head over to the

discount grocery store and buy a hefty, seedy, two-pound zucchini for a dollar. And this starts to hint at the difference
between food as sustenance and food as pleasure. Why pay
more for less? And on my side of the equation, why grow
less for more money—why nip a zucchini in the bud at two
inches when, given a few days, it will grow into a higher calo-
rie, more affordable option? Isn't that on some level wasteful,
even frivolous?

No, it isn't, for several reasons. First and most importantly,
specialty foods help small-scale local farmers earn a living. In
turn, these farmers provide valuable services to the community
that out-of-town corporate farms do not, such as food security; a reservoir of local knowledge; an infusion of dollars into
the local economy; and fresher, more nutritive, and potentially
more environmentally friendly produce.

Second, I'm not sure that the branding of the farmers'
markets as an elite and frivolous place to shop is appropriate at all. While we do sell specialty baby produce, we also
offer standard-size, competitively priced fare. In fact, much of
the produce you find at our farmers' market is being sold for
equal or even lesser cost than the supermarket equivalent. The
idea that everything is more expensive at farmers' markets is a
myth, perpetuated largely, it seems, by people who don't actually shop at farmers' markets.

At our farm stand, we tried to strike a balance between
specialty and standard items. Throughout the season, we price-
checked our produce at local grocery stores, and although we
may not have been able to match the price of a bargain basement sale, we were consistently competitive with mid-range
stores. And of course, some of the more unusual foods that
we sold couldn't be found at a store. If prices for these specialty items seemed high, it was because they helped to balance

things out, reflecting a living (or almost living) wage for the farmer who grew them.*

We were lucky to be able to sell our produce directly to the people who would consume it. Farmers selling products indirectly—that is, wholesale to grocery stores and most restaurants**—earn so little per item that the scale of the farm must be massive in order to earn any money at all. If I made six cents for every dollar's worth of produce I sold, I don't want to even think about what my hourly wage would be—but that's the way it goes for most farmers. The produce that they work so hard to cultivate is eventually sold to a customer for nearly twenty times what the farmer was paid for it. Under this system, my two-acre farm would be a patch of earth into which I'd pour money with a hearty negative return for my troubles.

So in order for me to compete with the grocery stores, which have many advantages over the farmers' market— variety, round-the-clock hours, out-of-season produce, refrigerators and misting systems—it is exceptionally helpful for me to carry things that they can't. Like itty-bitty squash with the blossoms still attached. Or unusual heritage varieties of summer squash, like Romanesco, which originates in Italy and is judged by many chefs to have the most flavorful flesh of any of the summer squashes. But like many heirloom varieties, Romanesco is not a widely produced commercial crop. When it comes to heirloom produce, my small size and local focus help me beat out the large-scale commercial farms, who don't

---

*If eggs (mentioned in Chapter 3) are more expensive than grocery store eggs, it is because the price reflects a humane standard for the hen as well as the cost of locally purchased, organic feed—money that goes to support local feed stores and employees. As excited as I was about earning money from eggs, our flock essentially breaks even.

**In Healdsburg, the farmers' market is a regular stop for several local chefs who pay full market price for produce.

grow heirlooms for reasons ranging from transportability and rate of ripening to cost and availability of seeds. So baby foods and heirloom varieties—the things that critics love to brand as highfalutin—are important to the small farm's ability to compete with megafarms and thus earn a living.

And even our standard produce offered other benefits that the grocery store couldn't. Our vegetables were picked hours before being set out on display; all else being equal, they were still fresher and nutritionally superior to the same vegetables from a grocery chain. Studies have shown that broccoli that has been in transit for two weeks has lost most of its vitamin C and almost all of its calcium, iron, and potassium by the time the time it gets to your plate.[32] Plus, our produce had a personal story. We could talk about how and when our produce was grown; the faceless, farmerless produce stacked under the thunderstorm misters at the supermarket could not.

It's fundamentally silly to call local farmers' markets elite, although an odd (and to my mind, rather mean-spirited) backlash has done so. Significant portions of our economy—the $247 million spent each year on golf shoes,[33] the $2 billion per year spent on chewing gum[34]—rely on entirely frivolous pursuits, and yet we typically do not begrudge the jobs they create. Few jobs today directly result in the production of life-giving necessities. The talk show host who criticizes farmers' marketers should apply the same level of criticism to his or her own job. Or, if a farmers' market critic has ever bought a bouquet of flowers—which is an expensive, useless item that is already dead and will be more obviously so in a week—then he or she is acquiring a product much further out of the reach of poor Americans than my vegetables. One doesn't typically accuse cell phone users of taking part in an elite hobby, yet for years human society functioned perfectly well without the ability to talk to a long-distance friend and order a latte at the same time. Humans have, however, always required food. And historically, that food has been grown by individuals from the local community.

When push comes to shove, farmers' marketers grow food for our immediate community. There is no task more essential. If you want to get slightly paranoid about it, grocery stores have one of the highest inventory turnover rates of any store; the entire inventory turns over an average of 12.7 times per year.[35] In other words, if the food chain were disrupted, *everything* would be gone from grocery store shelves in less than a month; local farms and backyard gardens would offer the only source of nutrition. The frightening thing is there wouldn't be nearly enough local farms to supply rural towns, let alone big cities. Even the tiniest towns in the middle of nowhere would struggle to find enough food, surrounded as they are by monocrops. A body cannot thrive on corn alone, especially if it's livestock corn destined for feedlots thousands of miles away.

And if the diverse foods we offer can be labeled elite, they can also be called traditional. They're the taste of the home garden—which, before food production became a standardized commercial activity, was the purveyor for peasants as well as palaces. A peasant could harvest and fry up male zucchini flowers—those flowers on the plant that are for pollination purposes only, and will never turn into fruit—as easily as the king's chef could. But since luminous orange squash blossoms are extremely perishable, they can't be commercially produced. As the logic goes, if an item can't be commercially produced, it will be more expensive; therefore, it's foodie food, not real people food.

To which I say: Please. These blossoms are fifty cents apiece. You'd be hard-pressed to find *anything* in the check-out line of the grocery store priced at fifty cents. And if you did, I'm guessing that first of all, it's on sale—and is likely being sold at cost. And secondly, no human hand ever touched it—your fifty-cent edible trinket is the product of an advanced factory system in which one human oversees a host of machines employed to perform the fundamental human task of making food.

But if you forgo your candy bar to buy one of my squash blossoms, you are employing me to feed you, to take loving care of a small plot of ground just down the road, and to know the essential hows of food: how to grow it, how to harvest it, and how to cook it. You're paying me to carry on tradition, and you're paying me to carry knowledge that some day you might require, should you ever decide to plant squash on your own.

The heirloom Armenian cucumbers we grew and sold at the market couldn't be found at an average grocery store.

(Though the ingredients of edible trinkets are closely guarded trade secrets, farmers tend to be far less monopolistic. We sell starts in spring for customers to plant in their own gardens, and we're always ready to answer questions about backyard growing.) I'm your personal farmer, providing you with the same quality food that humans have grown for hundreds and even thousands of years.

So if certain farmers' market produce is slightly more expensive than grocery store fare on a per-calorie basis, that's because the cost reflects the effort of a diversified growing process. Grocery stores can afford to not make money on certain items because a sale brings in customers, and encourages them to spend more money on other profit-making items (particularly processed foods). If I took this approach, I would be working sixty to eighty hours a week for nothing.

Well, I guess I'd be working sixty to eighty hours a week for the privilege of squash rash, cracked fingers, stained hands, an achy back, and a bad tan. For too few showers, filthy fingernails, and torn pants and shirts.

I may have missed my five-year high school reunion, but I knew where my peers were. Business school, law school, med school; at banks and firms and start-ups in New York, San Francisco, and Los Angeles. If you measure success in salaries, cars, and clothes, I am hardly elite; in fact, I lose handily. Stock options and IRAs aren't part of my job description. I don't own a suit. At the moment, I was living off of savings and the generosity of my boyfriend's parents, hoping that some day two risks would pay off—the financial risk of starting up a farm business from scratch, and the far more terrifying risk that my first multiyear relationship could also be my last. That maybe, after four years of dating and three of living together, we would make it official—so that when customers searched for the right word to describe Emmett, I wouldn't have to fill in with that all-too-shallow word "boyfriend" or the awkward "partner," which may have had an appropriate denotation but connoted a strictly professional relationship, the presence of a cowboy, or the existence of a gay lover, none of which applied to us.

Instead, I remained the would-be farmer's long-term girlfriend. And my odds for an imminent change of status didn't seem good. Granted, we had, in private, told each other that we wanted to spend the rest of our lives together, but at some point the rest of the world needed to know this. Sure, we'd started to appear in one another's family photos, and it was generally assumed that when we were invited to functions, our other half would be coming along for the ride. But words matter, and few are so public as *husband* and *wife*. There's something about marriage that says: I choose you to be my family, I choose you to be my home. And there's something about society that recognizes and even honors this choice despite all cynicism and pessimism to the contrary.

It pissed me off that I wanted to marry him. I was never the girl who dreamed of marrying the boy, and in fact I really never thought much about marriage—aside from a deeply rooted desire to avoid my parents' disastrous version—until now. But while I didn't want to "get married" per se, I wanted to marry Emmett. I very nearly proposed to him at a remote hot spring on the Olympic Peninsula after a hard hike up a mountain, when the light was soft and the whole green world empty of humanity. I told him that later in New Zealand, one late night in our van, hoping that maybe he'd get the hint.

Emmett got the hint just fine, but he wasn't ready and didn't really see the need to marry. You know, since we were already planning on spending the rest of our lives together anyway. Besides, he didn't really want to find himself in the awkward position of being the first of his close-knit cousins to marry. Why this position could be considered awkward, I hadn't the slightest idea, but Emmett's never been one to draw attention to himself.

I glanced over at Emmett, counting the bills. It was noon. For the time being, I'd pack up the remaining produce, save some for the local food pantry, and feed the rest to my flock of awkward teenage chickens. That night I'd dip squash blossoms in batter and fry them up for supper, with a side of sautéed beans: peasant food. When I climbed into bed, arms itching and shoulders stinging with sunburn, I'd realize he was no longer an aspiring farmer. I'd roll over and say goodnight with the traditional blown kiss; he'd catch it, send one back. And I wouldn't have to wonder what I actually accomplished that day. Every part of my farmer's body would already know.

Chapter 6

BAGS AND BAGS

······································

Beans

At the Healdsburg farmers' market, three large wicker baskets brimmed with beans. They were arranged in stripes of color: one basket filled with green Kentucky Wonders; one basket half green with Blue Lakes and half purple with Royal Burgundies; the third basket strikingly split between dark Dow Purple Pod pole beans and lustrous yellow wax beans.

The baskets were overfull, heaped high. The beans within them were uniformly young and tender, of a smaller size than those offered by other market stands. No doubt about it: I was starting to assume an air of legitimacy. It was looking like I might be able to do more than kill things—maybe, just maybe, I could grow them, too.

I was beaming over my bean bounty when a tourist couple stopped by.

"Would you look at that!" a big-haired lady exclaimed, tugging on her husband's Hawaiian shirtsleeves (which tourists tend to sport in California despite the fact that they've stopped a few thousand nautical miles shy of Oahu). "I've never seen beans like *those* before." She stepped up to the baskets and fixed her eyes on me. "What do they taste like?"

"You can try one, if you like them raw," I replied. It was the purple that she was talking about: I plucked a small, tender, plum-colored bean pod from the basket and held it out to her. When a twist of her lip suggested that she wasn't partial to uncooked beans, I shrugged and bit into it. "They're similar to green beans in flavor, although many of our customers agree they're a bit sweeter than the greens."

"Wouldn't that look just lovely in a salad," she said, glancing around for a plastic bag.

With that, it was time for my standard honesty-is-the-best-policy caveat. "Just so you know, the purple beans gradually turn green as you cook them. Not the same color as a regular green bean—more of a blue-green. But depending on how long you cook them, you can end up with a purple-green tie-dyed effect that's quite nice."

"Interesting," she said, with an undertone of *only in California*. "Are they all the same price?"

"Four dollars a pound, mix and match."

The customer selected a quarter pound of Dow Purple Pod pole beans, a quarter pound of yellow wax beans, and a few Kentucky Wonders. She grabbed two bunches of Swiss chard, handed me five dollars, and continued on her way.

My tourist customer rated about average on the excitement scale. Many shoppers were familiar only with grocery store green beans; our bright display of yellow, purple, and two different varieties of green beans hooked them. Curious, they'd ask questions about flavor, texture, and length of cooking (purple beans are slightly sweeter; yellow wax, slightly more tender; and the different bean varieties cook at similar rates). If these moderately excited customers occupied the upper end of the income spectrum, they wouldn't hesitate to throw together a big bag of all the different varieties—and grab some summer squash, salad mix, and French Breakfast radishes while they were at it. If their budgets were a bit tighter, they'd spring for a small sampler—a little of this and a little of that—and one of our cheaper items, like Swiss chard. Either way, they probably wouldn't have stopped at our stand at all if they hadn't been drawn in by the beans—so the beans not only sold themselves, they also sold whatever other produce these customers happened to pick up. I'm not afraid to admit it: I was a Royal Burgundy bean pimp, using these lookers to hook customers, reel them in, and redirect them to slightly less exotic varieties.

Then there were the customers whose admiration of beans surpassed even my own. Often, these folks' parents or grandparents once trellised purple beans in the backyard. They'd never been able to find those beans in grocery stores; my offerings brought them the bright taste of memory, a sense of

We transformed from the bug-munched salad stall into a legitimate farm stand at the Healdsburg farmers' market.

heritage, the opposite of loss. One visit from these customers was enough to rekindle anybody's agrarian idealism—I was able to feel as though I was part of something greater than this small farmers' market, some return to a pre-prepackaging Golden Age.

Finally, there were the "beans are beans" customers. These constituted my least favorite group. They didn't particularly care what type of beans I was growing or how I grew them. They were unimpressed by the small size of the beans, harvested when young and tender. The one thing that they cared about was the fact that my beans cost four dollars per pound.

It was one thing if these customers were quiet, but a vocal "beans are beans" customer could ruin my entire day. The week before in Windsor—a more meat-and-potatoes town than Healdsburg, and consequently a tougher sell at the market— a man walked up to the stand, admired my beans, and then asked me the price.

When I told him, he scowled. "You've got to be kidding me. Four dollars a pound for *beans?*" He spat the word out with disdain.

I paused, unsure how to respond. Then I remembered. "At Whole Foods, they're selling purple beans for five dollars per pound."

"Well, I don't *shop* at Whole Foods," he snapped back, and his sneering remark was so full of retribution it bordered on hateful. He stalked off, and I didn't have the heart to respond. (Although I did spend the rest of the market thinking up my best comeback: "If you're making minimum wage at your job, sir, you're doing better than me.")

Are beans just beans? First of all, I take issue with the concept of "just beans." Rhetorically speaking, our society doesn't hold the bean in particularly high regard. The *Oxford English*

Dictionary lists the third definition of beans as "a very small amount or nothing at all," while *Merriam-Webster* states the second definition simply as "a valueless item." Beans pop up in various clichés, too. Those who make beans for a living make little. In English and Australian usage, to "not have a bean" is to be broke. In France, *fin des haricots* (literally "the end of the beans") is an apocalyptic phrase my mother would summarize as "up shit creek without a paddle." If even the beans have run out, good luck to you, sir.

Common parlance subconsciously pits the customer against four-dollar-per-pound beans. And it's the gastronomic history of the bean that has produced this linguistic bias: beans were, and still are, peasant protein. Those who can afford to dine on meat, do. Those who can't, eat beans.

The bean-eating societal distinction dates back to feudal Europe. The landed class possessed the ability to graze herds of cattle and sheep, or to hunt game on horseback. Those without land were forced to eat more economically, obtaining protein from sources that required a fraction of the growing space. In a time when class distinctions were stark and cruel, beans became indelibly associated with poverty: the stigma of the "poor man's meat" was born. Even today, legumes remain a staple of impoverished people, overpopulated regions, or areas with scant grazing land.

In fact, beans are still at the forefront of international class differences. America is the land of hamburgers. The U.K. is the land of roast (or corned) beef, France of filet mignon, New Zealand of lamb, Australia of outback steaks, Germany of sausage. In developed nations, the dish du jour is usually meat. But throughout much of the third world—particularly in Asia and South America—meals often center around some variety of bean. (The black and pinto beans of South America are, at the species level, taxonomically identical to the heritage beans I grow.) As developing nations narrow the gap between the third world and the first, economists note that they typically undergo a "meat revolution." In other words, as soon as the residents of developing nations have access to disposable income, their diets shift abruptly away from beans and grains. That first bite into a thick, juicy steak offers not just gustatory pleasure, but also the sense of having arrived: in the twenty-first century, the ability to consume meat still represents a giant leap up the social ladder.

But despite the peasant stereotype, beans harbor a certain nobility. If you strip away the pall of history and examine the bean through a biological lens, you'll find that its unique abilities demand a gardener's reverence. From the moment it emerges from the soil, the bean is in a class all its own.

Well, to be taxonomically correct, the bean is actually in a family all its own. Fabaceae, the legume family, is unique in its ability to influence the planet's crucial nitrogen cycle.

All creatures—plant, animal, or otherwise—require nitrogen. Nitrogen compounds form the basis of proteins and nucleic acids, the very building blocks of life and reproduction. The air we breathe is 78 percent nitrogen, so you'd think we earthlings would have it pretty good. But that massive reservoir of gaseous N_2 is inaccessible to the likes of you and me. We can uptake our nitrogen only from plants or from animals that have dined on plants. And plants, in order to process nitrogen, need it to be "fixed" first—that is, made into a bioavailable compound (one that contains either oxygen or hydrogen).

Which is where legumes come in. As a legume grows, its roots are invaded by *Rhizobium*, a commonly occurring soil bacterium. Once established, *Rhizobium* multiplies like mad, forming bumpy nodules on the fibrous roots—a most welcome disease. The plant encourages *Rhizobium* by supplying it with energy and nutrients; *Rhizobium* responds in kind, bequeathing the plant with ammonium, a bioavailable form of nitrogen.* Thus, because they've got their own portable fertilizer, legumes have the handy-dandy ability to colonize nitrogen-poor soils. When the legume dies and decomposes, nitrogen is re-released into the soil—providing a friendlier sprouting environment for future plant inhabitants.

Because of its special *Rhizobium* relationship, gardeners use members of the Fabacaea family as a winter cover crop, plowing them under in spring to add nitrogen to the soil. Or, if they're rotating crops in succession, farmers will plant beans after a heavy feeder like corn because beans will produce amply even in nitrogen-depleted soil.

And the legume is as beautiful as it is useful. The pole bean rears his little head—seed-noggin, leaf-ears—out of the crusty clay soil and instantly demands attention. This is a bold seedling, tall and sturdy, yet the youngster politely tucks his leaves down at night and raises them to greet each morning with a fine sun salutation. As he grows, he inscribes patterns against the blue sky, twining irregularly around whatever happens to be in his path, leaving loud cursive loops leading to the runner's final serif.

There's something a bit dark about the legume, too—especially in the context of an entire row of beans. They clamber up each other, grappling desperately for light, using other things to support themselves rather than developing a strong enough stem on their own. But if it's dark it's also beautiful: the evolutionary efficiency, the speed of growth, the brilliance of the bean's swaying dance that leads it to twine around

---

Interestingly, termites—which subsist on a nitrogen-poor diet of dead wood—have established a parallel relationship with nitrogen-fixing diazotrophs that live in their guts.

objects. A marvelous adaptation—like the strangler fig, gorgeously sinister.

And, like a peasant, the bean seedling needs no coddling. He's tender, perhaps, but he's born with an ability to function. If cucumber beetles attack his first two leaves, he has energy enough to put out two more—and another, and another, until the bugs can't possibly keep up. By comparison, the tinier seeds of the plant world—onions, carrots—emerge more like marsupials. They're so fragile that they must be pampered, endlessly weeded and watered. The bean? He's grateful if you pull out the weeds, but he'll outgrow them even if you don't.

Which is why "full of beans" is appropriate. The phrase originally referred to someone who, like a manly peasant worker, brims with energy. Of all the clichés, this one fits the plant best.

. . . .

At the moment, I was very full of beans. In fact, I was a little past full—and despite my proud smiles at the farmers' market, back at the field my enthusiasm for the prolific legume was running on empty.

As usual, I'd been the original enthusiast for the too-big-for-our-britches endeavor. I insisted that we plant five different heirloom varieties of beans, urging at least one hundred row-feet of the crop. When we experienced a near-perfect germination rate, I airily dismissed the concept of thinning the seedlings. Each one was so valiant, so artistic—how could we possibly get rid of any?

And so I was the only one to blame when the plants that started out so lithe and graceful rapidly grew into an insurmountable thicket.

At first, I was a little bit proud of my bean jungle. It was magnificent, a peasant hedge fit for a king: ten feet tall, three feet deep, and practically impenetrable to light. Unfortunately it blocked the tomatoes' afternoon sun. I reasoned that the loss of ripe tomatoes would be offset by a plenitude of beans. After all, beans and tomatoes sell for approximately the same price per pound—no harm done.

That sort of reasoning predated the Great Bean Revelation.

The revelation took place on a Friday, our first real bean harvest, at the time when miracles happen on farms—when the farmer stops hoeing, sowing, and weeding, and instead devotes his waking hours to reaping. Zucchini can't be contained. Cherry tomatoes ripen at breakneck speed, the heirlooms are swelling and yellowing, crookneck squash form a snake's nest, and if the Armenian cucumbers aren't harvested every other day, there's going to be hell to pay.

And on this Friday, in the midst of a veritable harvest festival, Emmett and I turned our attention to the bean thicket. Eying our tall, dark nemesis, we each grabbed a bin and headed to the shady side of the row. The lush bean vines protected us from the sun—but the lush bean vines also hid the bean pods inside their green folds. Picking beans is an intimate endeavor and the plant seems to like the attention. Its furred leaves cling to clothing, leaving farmers festooned with green spades.

An hour later, sticky with sweat, I stepped back to see what we'd accomplished. Between the two of us, we had managed to (mostly) harvest (a bit less than) one half of one row. There were three rows. We had harvested probably a thousand beans—which added up to a mere bin.

At this point, I was sweaty, tired, and humbled by the bean. What a bounty of food, what a phenomenal ability to proliferate one's offspring. For each bean pod we picked

The bean tendrils meandered as they reached for the sky.

would, if we'd let them develop further, produce several bean seeds capable of creating new plants. If each plant produced one hundred pods (a conservative estimate), that would easily be five hundred potential progeny.

And so my awe came with a healthy dollop of fear.

Here's the thing: it takes one good tomato to add up to a pound. The harvesting effort required is at most thirty seconds to locate the tomato, snip it off, and place it in the box. In contrast, a person must pick close to one hundred beans to add up to one pound. Instead of thirty seconds of work, it's more like ten minutes.

And so I began to resent the beans. *Especially* for shading out the tomato plants. Emmett resented them because they gave him a rash. He lay in bed at night, scratching his hands, forearms, biceps, the back of his neck—resenting *me* because I hadn't permitted the bean thinning, a move that would have diminished rash potential. And pretty soon, we both resented the fact that in order to stay on top of the beans, we had to harvest them for several hours every day. In August, which in Sonoma County means hundred-degree weather. While the cucumbers could, in a pinch, be kept at bay with a twice- or thrice-weekly harvest, the beans wouldn't wait that long. I'd blink and suddenly my tender Dow Purple Pod pole beans would be grossly elongated and podded out, suitable only to shuck for soup beans.

This was a conundrum we hadn't anticipated back when we were killing hundreds of seedlings and wondering whether we had enough produce to take to market. Too much produce? The thought was absurd. But as economists and food system analysts love to say, there is no food shortage on this planet—there's just a distribution problem. Globally, 4.3 pounds of food are produced for every man, woman, and child per day: more than enough to satisfy everyone.[36]

Still, I assumed that the distribution problem took place elsewhere. It was global. America had too much, Africa too little. And if we *were* considering a national scale, surely the distribution gap took place in the massive, subsidized cornfields of the Midwest—not on a tiny, two-acre Californian farm run by two novice farmers who only recently learned the proper way to plant a potato.

And yet Foggy River Farm had become part of the economists' scenario. It wasn't just the beans, either—it was everything. Our little postage stamp was bursting at the seams. We couldn't sell all the produce, let alone eat it.

Our initial solution had been the local food pantry. They gladly accepted our cucumbers, beans, and summer squash, but drew the line at chard and kale. Not a popularity contest, mind you—although chard and kale would lose that handily— it was just that they didn't have sufficient refrigerator capacity, so they only accepted produce that would be okay for twenty-four hours or so unrefrigerated. But the food pantry wasn't open on the weekends, when it would be convenient to stop by on the way home from the farmers' market. We had to deliver on Mondays, which were one of our busiest field days (since we'd spent our weekend at the farmers' markets, mostly away from the field). And, all do-gooder, warm feelings aside, the stress of constantly harvesting and driving to the edge of town to give away the produce that we were trying to make a living from was starting to take its toll on us.

In the beginning, I was as excited as the pastor who received our several pounds of heirloom beans at the Food Pantry every Monday. On weekday mornings, I'd pick the west side of the pole bean rows, marveling at the productivity of the different varieties: Kentucky Wonders, Blue Lakes, and Dow Purple Pod pole beans, the earliest and biggest producer of all. I'd crouch down to pluck the pods of the bush beans—yellow wax, pale and tender, Royal Burgundy, curved and dark. In the afternoons, Emmett and I would patrol the east side of the bean rows, hiding always from the onslaught of the sun.

Morning beans, afternoon beans—and beans featured prominently at dinnertime, too. In those early days, I couldn't contain my delight at their flavor, sautéed with a bit of olive oil and garlic, seasoned with sea salt and black pepper and perhaps a splash of balsalmic vinegar or the squeeze of a Meyer lemon, just at the end.

But the bounty was quickly turning into an all-out produce profusion. And while we did have a few too many cucumbers, crookneck squash, and chard leaves, our angst centered around the beans. The once-treasured beans, the once-poeticized beans, the once shake-your-moneymaker gourmet beans now engendered a certain level of vitriol in our hearts.

Emmett, unfortunately, had been cast in the role of Enforcer—the person who, day after day, reminded me that it was once again time to pick the beans. This left me to play the Dennis the Menace, "Awww, shucks, not again" character. When bribing didn't work ("Hey mister, want some gelato?"), I dragged my feet like a petulant preschooler all the way to the field.

Emmett began, "Really, when it comes to the beans, I'm just about ready to . . ."

I jumped in: "Rip them all out and burn them?"

. . . .

To be fair, the beans did not entirely choke out our heirloom tomato harvest. They merely slowed it down. In mid-August, as the first of our heirloom tomatoes readied themselves, we harvested the ripest ones the evening before market and arranged them carefully in cardboard fruit boxes we'd picked up at a local grocery store. Compared to bean harvesting, tomato picking was a breeze—the fruit piled up quickly. Unlike beans, however, it required a deft touch.

Our heirloom tomatoes were staked, tied onto wooden poles with lengths of stretchy green plastic. And here's the thing about heirlooms: if they're not diseased, split, moldy, stunted, punctured, sun scalded, infested by ants, or prematurely gnawed by overeager deer/rodents/teenagers, then chances are they're stuck between the vine and the stake. The biggest, most beautiful ones are of course the most likely to be inextricable, which means that after several frustrating minutes of trying to gently pull them out from every possible angle, you will inevitably go for the big yank technique, impaling the most beautiful tomato in the world on its own vine. Of course, the moment the tomato has been mortally punctured, the offending vine will once again seem soft and pliable, and you'll never quite figure out exactly what part of the vine inflicted the wound—a mystery no doubt related to its nightshade witchcraft roots. Edible wolf-peach, indeed.

In my sweaty hand was a fatally wounded Cherokee Purple. *Damn*, I thought, and then, *More bruschetta for us.*

As Emmett and I filled the fruit boxes, they transformed from a drab cardboard backdrop to a lively mosaic of red, purple, orange, yellow, and green. It was spectacular, this splash of summer, and the sheer number of plants meant that our failures were not nearly as important as they would have been if we were only tending a few bushes in the backyard. We could take a hit, lose five plants, pass over the sunburned, wormy fruits, suffer through the shade of the bean trees, and still bring three cardboard boxes full of plump fruit to the farmers' market.

Correction: Two cardboard boxes full of plump fruit to the farmers' market. In the morning, when we peeked in the tomato boxes as we loaded them into the car, more were lost. Overnight, the perfectly ripe tomatoes—which were not, by our estimation, overripe—had split. Tomatoes that were slightly overripe upon picking—those that had sported small splits but seemed saleable—had sprouted fuzzy gray mold. Three boxes shrank to two, but it didn't matter.

While we didn't quite rip out the bean hedge and burn the plants, part of the reason that I was able to stand at the farmers' market gleefully lording over my piles of beans—and our first display of heirloom tomatoes—was this: we had declared an end to the bean tyranny. We had decided to reduce our harvest to one row of beans. The rest would go to seed and dry for use in winter soup.

And for the next year, we had plans.

Plan number one: Don't plant beans next to the tomatoes like novice dolts. Plan number two: Plant them in succession, so there's always one group of beans at their peak. The beans are stringless and most tender early in their productivity cycle; later, they're quick to pod out and grow woody, which is partly why we found ourselves harvesting beans morning and night. Plan number three: Engage Leviticus. Plan number four: Get wwoofers.

Leviticus 23:22 reads, "When you reap the harvest of your land, do not reap to the very edges of your field or gather the gleanings of your harvest. Leave them for the poor and the alien." The spirit of this verse has inspired some charity groups (not all of whom are religious) to start up gleaning programs around the country. Many farmers, like us, leave some harvestable produce in the field—but these days, it's a bit of a faux pas to walk onto someone's land and start gathering their gleaning. It takes a helping hand to bring that produce to the poor and to the stranger.

The Society of Saint Andrews, which takes its name from the disciple who played an instrumental role in Jesus' miracle of the loaves and fishes, is the largest gleaning organization in the United States. According to organization spokeswoman

Carol Breitinger, they "salvage twenty to thirty million pounds of produce a year, and all that food either would have been plowed under in the field or dumped into the landfill. There's nothing wrong with it. It's just either commercially not marketable, because it is blemished or the wrong size or wrong shape, or it's excess."[37] In California alone, Society members gleaned and distributed 13.5 million pounds (or 40.5 million servings) of potatoes and other produce as part of the statewide Potato Project.[38]

In Sonoma County, there are three local gleaning organizations that take from the field to give to the poor: Farm to Pantry, Grateful Gleaners, and Petaluma Bounty. Dedicated individuals volunteer their time to harvest extra produce from farms and bring them to a local food pantry, or to take unsold farmers' market leftovers to soup kitchens. Next year, we hoped to invite the Healdsburg-based Farm to Pantry to glean our off-peak beans. It would take the pressure off us at a time when we really didn't have extra hours to spend harvesting food that wouldn't bring income but would still give valuable calories to folks who needed them.

While it's spiritually sound to commit a portion of one's produce to the less fortunate, there's also something to be said for maintaining economic viability. And for small-scale organic farmers, there's a second, more economically beneficial way to deal with overabundance: exchange it for free labor. Economists might insist that there's no such thing as a free lunch, but at WWOOF (Willing Workers On Organic Farms*) that axiom simply doesn't hold true.

---

*WWOOF is also referred to as World Wide Opportunities on Organic Farms, a name that developed to avoid confusion in immigration offices as to whether wwoofers were migrant workers or tourists on holiday.

The philosophy of WWOOF is simple. The organization establishes approximate ground rules for a labor exchange: half a day's work in return for food and lodging. For a suggested donation of five dollars, farmers can publish information about their farm in a WWOOF guide (also available online). Interested "wwoofers"—typically young travelers—then contact the hosting farmers to determine availability. If all goes well, a host will receive four free hours of work each day. The wwoofer will receive a free bed and food—with enough time off to explore the surrounding areas. The relationship between wwoofer and farmer can last for as little as a few days, or as long as a year. It's usually a sociable learning experience, with wwoofers and hosts exchanging not just goods and services but knowledge: farming technique, conversation, and travel stories. And wwoofers can improve the profitability of a small farm: with extra hands to harvest, a farmer who normally sells only at farmers' markets could, for instance, branch out into wholesale, selling to restaurants or local grocery stores that pay the farmer less than direct market transactions. For some farmers, profit margins are so thin that they can't afford to sell to these less lucrative markets. But if they have free labor, they can.

While this sounds like an ideal situation, there's obviously a considerable amount of trust involved. A farmer is inviting a complete stranger into his or her home; a wwoofer is sleeping in the home of a complete stranger. Surely something this foolhardy only takes place in socialist-leaning countries like Sweden or open, devil-may-care countries like Australia. Or the decorous, tea-loving countryside of England, where the organization formed back in 1971.

Yet there are currently 4,727 registered wwoofers in the United States, with an average of 393 new members each month. There are 800 host farms here, 112 in California alone.[39]

Granted, New Zealand (a country with 1 percent of our population) boasts over 1,000 host farms. But still, 800 trusting American households is nothing to scoff at. And interestingly, while most wwoofers in New Zealand are international travelers, many of the wwoofers here are U.S. citizens looking to learn more about their own country.

For us, hosting a wwoofer would also be a way of giving back to the agricultural community. For five months, we had "wwoofed" our way around New Zealand, developing skills and techniques that would serve us well when we returned home to start our own farm. The generosity and knowledge base of the host farmers astounded us; we'd both enjoy the opportunity to follow in the footsteps of our hosts by showering a wwoofer with fresh, home-cooked meals and pointers about local spots to visit.

. . . .

At the market, as I put away our unsold leftovers at closing time, I was hatching yet another plan. The day's leftovers included one and a half bins of chard, one of kale, a few pounds of crookneck squash, a handful of Patty Pans, several pounds of green beans, and just a few tomatoes. The flower guy stopped by to give us a bouquet in exchange for squash and chard; Emmett headed over to the bread seller to see what he'd like from us in return for a loaf of whole grain bread.

Trading is one positive aspect to market leftovers—we ended up with everything from breads and cheeses to walnuts and onions—but no matter how hard we tried, we couldn't trade away everything. The freshly picked bouquets of rainbow chard, pert and voluminous, arranged with careful attention to color and size, broke my heart. By this evening, they'd have met their final resting place on the compost pile, withering with the weeds. The chicks weren't quite ready to tackle the amount of produce we had on hand—for that, we'd need full-grown poultry, and judging by our quantities, possibly more than thirty girls.

As I dropped the last crooknecks into a bag and twist-tied the end closed, I decided that there had to be a better way. Wouldn't it be great to have a guaranteed produce sale—and, in the case of a surplus, the ability to give loyal customers free extras?

And so I began charting the lines of my argument to convince Emmett that next year, Foggy River Farm should really start a CSA (Community Supported Agriculture) program. And maybe a U-Pick bean operation, and WWOOF hosting, and a work-trade program, and weekly gleaning, too.

But in the meantime, there would be many nights of farmers' market feasting. The star of the season had arrived. And while the proletariat bean failed to overthrow it, I would be the final conqueror, the proof in the blade of my bread knife buried tonight deep in a Striped German. As I watched the seeds spill out of the tomato cavity, I'd laugh out loud: I'm going to eat this tomato, and I'm going to like it.

Chapter 7

WORM FRIENDLY

....

Sweet Corn

"Two ears?" I asked, incredulous. "All this for two lousy ears? You have to be kidding."

"Be grateful," Emmett said. "It used to be one or two, now it's two or three."

I was standing by a plant that dwarfed me. It towered six feet tall; elongated emerald-green leaves sprayed out from the central stalk, which culminated in a wheaten broom—a sort-of angel atop a sort-of tree.

Affixed to this giant plant were precisely two ears of corn. The ears, enveloped in green, were accented by dun fibers protruding from their tips.

"I think it's ready," Emmett said. "The book says that when the tip of the ear is filled out and firm, it's sweet."

With that announcement, he ripped an ear from the stalk. It was more like removing a branch, really; it didn't just pop off neatly, but rent with a sound like the breaking of bones. Or perhaps cartilage—the same sound as that of a turkey drumstick being removed.

Emmett pulled back the fibrous green casing with a squeak, but someone had beaten him to the corn's sweet kernels. One fat, green worm had munched a thick trail halfway down the cob, leaving an ugly brown cavity in its wake.

Unfazed, Emmett stepped deeper into the corn jungle and wrenched an ear off a different plant. Two worms, a quarter of the way down the ear. A third ear: three worms, still young and clustered near the top. After six ears—all of which had at least one worm—Emmett consented to acknowledge the trend.

I thought the words but did not say them aloud that time. *Crop failure.* Instead, I played the Pollyanna card.

"Well, the chickens will love all this corn."

"I didn't grow all this corn for *chickens.*"

"Well, they'll enjoy the worms, anyway."

Emmett scowled. As he gazed down the long rows at our multiple successions of corn—each block out from us one week less mature than the one before—he wasn't ready to give up just yet. He bit into one, just to prove his point.

"It tastes fine—it's not like the whole cob is ruined. On most of them, the worm's not too far down. We can still sell these," he said, and paused. "Maybe for a small discount."

First of all, I wasn't sure our statistically insignificant sampling of corn granted us the authority to say that most of the worms were contained in the top section of the ear. And secondly, I wasn't sure that Emmett's judgment mirrored the general population's when it came to the palatability of food. I love the man and his garbage-disposal skills that enable him to finish off whatever's left on my plate—but sometimes he eats things I'd rather avoid touching, let alone put in my mouth. Suspect leftovers in the fridge? They smell a little funny, but they taste just fine. Every once in a while, he'll get halfway

Corn earworms dined on our cobs long before we could.

through an aged Tupperware supper and start to feel queasy. The queasiness—not the fact that the leftovers are two weeks old and I begged him not to eat them—is what finally makes him toss it in the trash. He's a big proponent of not letting things go to waste. While I agree with the concept, I'm not always comfortable with the extremity with which he puts it into practice.

Sweet, salted, and slathered in butter, I've always loved corn. But at the moment I couldn't possibly imagine why any farmer in her right mind would remotely consider growing this worthless, pest-infested, energy-intensive crop. It requires babying—ample nitrogen from compost, plenty of water, regular mounding of soil to prevent the shallow root systems from giving up and letting the whole plant topple over—but it doesn't provide much return for these efforts. One six-foot plant, producing its two paltry ears, is worth exactly one dollar.

If those ears are even saleable. And I was skeptical about how many customers would be willing to shell out good money for wormy corn when the local grocery store offered big, glistening heaps of the stuff without any unappetizing inhabitants. Come to think of it, sometimes the grocery store had corn on sale: four for a dollar. How was that even *possible*?

Cheap supermarket corn is partially made possible through the liberal application of pesticides. There are at least five worm-like critters that prey on sweet corn plants, and they're found across North America: the wireworm, the cutworm, the European corn borer, the fall armyworm. But of all the invaders, the most infamous is the corn earworm, which feeds directly on the market product and renders the corn unattractive, if not unmarketable. The earworm's persistence and ubiquity poses a serious threat to the corn grower; to quote a University of Kentucky entomologist: "Once worms have become established within the ear, control is impossible."[40]

The typical chemical program calls for spraying every three to five days from the time when the ears begin to form silks to the time when most of the silks have wilted. And for farms like ours—that have new blocks of corn maturing every week for continuous harvest—this would mean spraying every three to five days for most of the summer and into the fall. Biological control is also an option, with predators such as lacewings, minute pirate bugs, and damsel bugs all eager to dine on earworm eggs and small larvae. But on our farm, the cause of death of any given corn earworm is more likely to be kin than kith. Specifically, a corn earworm is more likely to be killed by another corn earworm than by an unrelated insect. In some fields, as many as 75 percent of the total corn earworms fall victim to cannibalism—which is why, when Emmett started shucking cobs, he tended to find either a few small earworms or one large one. First, the earworm eats the shell of the egg from which it hatched. Then it turns its attention to the corn kernels, then to its siblings, and then it eats its way out of the ear and pupates in the soil. Once it metamorphoses to the moth stage, the process begins again.

And so our little corner of the corn world on market day was full of worms. In the end, Emmett's optimism—his dogged insistence that a flaw really isn't a flaw, or maybe just that imperfection isn't the end of the world—overcame my disgust. Which is why this chilly Saturday morning air filled with grunts and bone-snapping sounds. Rip the branch off the corn-tree; snap the ear off the branch; toss the ear in a pile. Drumstick tear; grunt; pop; thud. Breathe.

....

At the Healdsburg farmers' market, we hauled out two gray plastic bins filled with corn and placed them on the market table. To one bin, we taped a paper sign: Worm-Friendly Corn. The words were accompanied by a hand-drawn sketch of a corn earworm. Emmett drew the worm hesitantly— unsure whether too much honesty made the best advertising policy—but even so, the wiggler had a certain panache: this wasn't some country worm, more like a city worm headed out on a hot date. I found the saucy invertebrate cute, artistic, and embarrassing as hell.

We finished setting up the booth early, which was unfortunate. We stared at the clever sign, the heaped corn, the green casings, some with escape holes drilled by exiting corn worms. By the time the market manager's bell pealed to signal the start of the day's sales, I was already blushing. The flash of heat across my cheeks took me a little by surprise: I hadn't expected a surge in self-consciousness so far into the season. But there I was, back at the beginning, a suburban slicker with weathered wares and a face that inevitably revealed too much.

There's intimacy in tending the plants that provide the food that people will lovingly prepare in some variation on a family ritual. In many places, farm work is purely mechanical, the end results bulk, the products shipped off to be consumed by unknown masses. But here, it's an art. And it feels like reading a formal poem in front of a classroom of students who have styled themselves after postmodern critics. Or like how I felt at the elementary school spelling bee when the judge asked me to spell the one word—out of all the words in the contest to that point—that I didn't recognize. I'm the girl who has to know how to spell the unfamiliar word; I'm the girl who has to know how to grow the vegetables. This is what I *do*, and I'm expected to do it well.

But I haven't; we haven't. Maybe it's impossible to grow aesthetically perfect corn without unleashing the wrath of the chemist on the corn maze. After all, much of the organic corn I've seen sold in the grocery store was shrink-wrapped in plastic, silky tips trimmed off. In other words, it may have been wormy too, but the corn had been shucked, cut, and shrink-wrapped so it could presented in a sterile, worm-free fashion to the customer. Even though the corn looked appealing, all the excessive packaging wasn't exactly an earth-friendly practice. Regardless, we didn't have any plastic wrap. Our corn had worms. All we could do was wait to see what people would do about it.

Moments after the market manager's bell rang, the results started rolling in. Corn, like the tomato, has a magnetic personality. Despite its sorry asking price, it's not like the bean—somehow it's a big-ticket item, a piece of produce people get excited about. Corn brings summer its sweetness: fresh from the farm, tossed in its husk on the barbecue next to sizzling sirloin steaks, it's an American icon (albeit—like the tomato— one pilfered from vanquished native peoples).

People caught sight of the ears piled high in the bins, wrapped tight in their green husks. And it was like something had hooked them. Eyes locked on the corn, they made a bee-line to our farm stand where, as if hypnotized, they tended to speak in sentences punctuated by exclamation points and question marks.

"Corn! When was it picked?"

"This morning," I answered. My customer's face lit up: she was practically licking her lips. And then she spotted the sign.

"Oooh, worm friendly, huh?"

At this point, her reaction could take one of two turns. The next thing that would happen would either be an under-standing chuckle, or a sort of shadow—ranging from uncer-tainty to outright revulsion—passing across her face. Then I'd know what type of customer I was dealing with.

"I think I'll pass."

The period deflated me. To avoid annihilation of my ego as a farmer and vendor, I had to take a bit of a moral high ground here. The way I looked at it, if there was one good thing about wormy corn, it was that it formed a test of mettle separating the girls from the women and the boys from the men. Really, if they couldn't handle a little worm, they didn't deserve farm-fresh, beyond organic, pesticide-free corn. Let them eat vacuum-packed corn from Mexico, doused in organic OMRI-certified pesticides. Or let them rifle through piles of picture-perfect, genetically modified corn, gene-spliced to resist herbicides and produce their own pesticides.

Meanwhile, I am proud to say that the corn worms were enhancing my farmer gal cred. Wormy corn was good for me. Far from my former squeamish, worm-hating self, I now flicked the little fuckers off the kernels with abandon. I was handy with the clippers, too, easily slicing through the thick cob to lop off the unsightly worm-eaten tips. Even at home, away from public scrutiny, corn worms now only elicited a reaction if I wasn't anticipating them. Or if I caught one munching on my ankle. You might not think it, but the little bastards actually bite.

And I wasn't the only one putting on a tough face at the farmers' market. In Healdsburg, courageous men and women—diehard customers of the local food system—scoffed at corn worms. The fact that our corn had worms made it more real, and these customers liked real food. "That's how I know it's not GMO!" they'd say, or "If it doesn't have worms, it isn't organic, is it?"

But there were also those customers who desperately wanted to support local farmers but would prefer to do it without acknowledging that organic farming involved lots of insects inhabiting the food they were about to ingest. These were the people who came up to the stand and waited awkwardly until it was their turn to confess: "I found a *bug* in your spring mix the other week."

Duh.

"I'm sorry, you know we do try our best to keep them out, but every once in a while one slips through."

"Well, I just thought I'd let you know. You know."

I know. Duh.

"Thanks! Well, I hope the salad was tasty, anyway."

"Oh, it was. We gave it a very thorough washing, and then it was delicious."

These people often requested that we remove the wormy bits before they'd purchase the corn. Obligingly, we did, although from an economic standpoint it clearly made no sense to spend several minutes husking and trimming items that we were offering for fifty cents apiece. But we did it, partly because we still felt a little depraved about selling wormy corn, and partly because I understood on a personal level how difficult it is to overcome worm phobias. I felt that it was my duty to extend a helping hand to those worm phobes with weaker constitutions than mine.

A particularly intriguing subset of the no-bug demographic was comprised of customers who didn't really believe in bugs in their salad or worms in their corn, but didn't really believe in killing them, either. This got complicated, especially when I pulled out the pruning shears to lop off the offending worm-eaten tip along with the offending worm.

"You're not going to kill it, are you?" one of our regular customers asked apprehensively.

"No, I'm just putting it in the bushes." Where, lacking its moist food source and protective husk, it would dehydrate and die, if it wasn't picked off by a bird or engulfed by ants before then.

"Oh good, I wouldn't want to hurt it."

This is the point where I was no longer on the same page as the customer—in fact, I was in an entirely different book, in a library on the other side of the world. I *did* want to hurt the worm. In fact, I wanted to hurt as many worms as possible. And I'd been a vegetarian for six years, so it wasn't like I didn't understand empathizing with animals. I wanted to ask, do you eat meat? If not, do you wash your hands, killing millions of innocent bacteria who are just trying to eke out a living and provide for the next generation? What would you do if five thousand ants invaded your refrigerator—let them eat cake? Really, we had to draw the line somewhere, and I can assure you there were thousands more of these worms in my field ready to replace the fallen hero.

Another regular customer walked up, a big grin plastered across his face at the sight of our corn. Later, I'd learn that he once worked on a farm in Haiti; he knows how these things go. "Worm friendly?" he mused. "I'll take eight!"

I'd throw in two extra, I told him—worm insurance. And with that, I'd set the hook. Even if a couple of the ears are worm cities, our worm insurance would ensure he'd be back at our farm stand looking for more next week.

. . . .

On the human menu for the evening: leftover sweet corn from the morning's market, paired with roasted new potatoes—dug that morning to check on the plants' progress—and roasted beets. On the avian menu for the evening: corn worms.

Now, the chickens weren't terribly adventurous yet. They were in the awkward teenage phase, which was every bit as bad in *Gallus gallus domesticus* as it is in *Homo sapiens*. They were leggy, scrawny, and covered in their adult feathers—but a few down feathers from chick-hood remained, reminding them that they weren't *really* adults just yet. Rather than pimples, sheathed feathers jutted up awkwardly from their skin. (I would imagine it would feel about as bad as a big zit, too; think about trying to push a feather tightly wrapped in fingernail out of one of your pores.) They spent a lot of their time preening themselves, trying to break through the keratin sheath to free the feather underneath. Their efforts rendered their rooms perpetually dirty, coating everything in the vicinity with a fine golden feather-dust. Their wattles and combs were, embarrassingly, just starting to swell and redden—the cockerels' more so than the pullets'. And, of course, they were starting to squabble and assert themselves, pushing their boundaries, discovering their personalities, and establishing social norms.

Up to this point, their diet had been limited to chick starter and a chard leaf or two. But today, they forayed into a new world: their first taste of flesh.

The original surviving seven chickens had already passed the ungainly phase. Now, just entering their prime, they inhabited the retrofitted chicken coop that had been safely floored with plywood to keep out predators. We'd also created a chicken yard by installing a chicken-wire fence. During the day, the gate would remain open, enabling the chickens to roam where they would. But at night, I'd shut the gate so the foxes wouldn't be able to get anywhere close to the coop: double security.

We hadn't yet introduced the awkward teenagers to the original chickens, and the reality of predation altered our coop plan. Originally we thought we'd have a dirt run "porch" attached to the chicken coop, to provide them with more space overnight. Now we realized that was just asking for trouble. So Emmett and I were working on a second, larger coop—but until it was done, our teenagers were spending their nights in the garage and their days in makeshift enclosures in the backyard (cardboard boxes artfully arranged to form an outer boundary, and old window screens placed on top so they didn't fly out and get eaten by the neighbor's dog).

Our dinner was almost ready, the roots browning in the oven, the water hot and the corn husked and trimmed, ready to go. We headed out into the yard with a handful of corn worms, slipped back the old window screen, and dropped in a fat green worm, which wriggled as it hit the ground.

The worm instantly became the focus of the flock's attention. The chickens stood around it awkwardly, sticking their necks out, turning their heads sideways and tilting them so that one eye squarely faced the ground. They studied the worm intently, yellow eyes blinking. For a half-minute they were practically frozen in place: a game of ring around the worm combined with freeze tag.

Suddenly a Rhode Island Red reacted. She took two steps up to the contorting worm, darted her head down quickly, and grasped it in her beak. And now, suddenly, everyone realized that worms were food—and not just any old food, but the best food they'd never tasted. As Red looked around nervously for an exit, the entire flock began to chase her. She darted back and forth, trying valiantly to keep her head away from the birds who were snapping at her beak, trying to deprive her of her prize. Her sisters were in hot pursuit until an evasive maneuver—running through them, rather than away—confused them momentarily.

Red had a split second to herself. She tilted back her head and gulped down the worm.

"Did you see that?" I asked Emmett. My heart was pounding at this little life-and-death game; the end was sudden, brutal. Somehow I'd imagined that the chickens would jointly peck the worm to death, each bird receiving a bit of a protein boost. I'd forgotten that chickens are not nearly that egalitarian— though they may not always be bloodthirsty cannibals, they are always bloodthirsty carnivores.

There was another reason my heart was pounding: when I was a kid, I had a friend who had a lizard. The lizard ate meal worms, until one day the meal worms ate the lizard. From the inside out. At least, that's what my friend told me. Now all I could think was: what if I just killed my chicken? The corn worms bite. What if I peered in the coop tomorrow to find a Rhode Island Red in her death throes, an evil fattened corn worm protruding from her neck? Shit, all the Rhode Island Reds looked the same; I couldn't even pick out the chicken who might be dead tomorrow.

As though I hadn't killed enough chickens already. Damn corn.

. . . .

Another characteristic corn shares with the tomato: corn is a touchy-feely food. People like to pick it up, squeeze it, pull the husk back. If we were charging full market price for corn, I'd feel less resentment at turning the other cheek—but we were already discounting *and* throwing in worm insurance for any-one who bought more than a couple of ears.

And still the customers heavy-handedly unsheathed our ears, showering all produce in the vicinity with corn silk (and, let's face it, corn worm poop), rejecting those they deemed unworthy. We quickly learned to place the corn bins on the ground, at the end of the stand, so that they didn't defile the rest of our display.

But shifting the mess to the parking lot asphalt solved only half the problem. Not only were we deworming ears, dis-counting our product, and giving some ears away—we were also ending up with half a bin full of the crummiest, wormiest corn at the end of the day.

Once again I found myself shaking my head at a bizarre societal norm. Why are we encouraged—with artfully placed trash cans—to shuck corn at the grocery store to see if it's up

We planted corn in blocks to maximize wind pollination.

to snuff, but forbidden to bite into an unpaid-for apple to find out if it's mushy or crisp? Why do customers feel it's okay to nab a few cherry tomatoes from the baskets that I sell, but not okay to take one stamp from the packs for sale at the post office to see if they like the way it sticks?

Oh well. At the very least, Emmett agreed, the wormtropolis leftovers could be used for chicken food. The trouble was, our chickens were only teenagers—and while they happily scarfed down several ears at a time, they couldn't handle thirty ears per day. Besides, sweet corn is mostly sugar. Chickens don't have any teeth to rot, but if we overloaded the teenagers with simple carbohydrates we'd have to increase their protein intake in some way. They were growing birds, and for optimum health they needed a diet that was about 20 percent protein; their bodies required more than corn carbs to build bones and muscle. Red junglefowl, the progenitor of the domesticated chicken, to this day thrives on a foraged diet in Southeast

Asia: bugs, grubs, seeds, and invertebrates. Although chickens' nutritional needs have, like the bird itself, evolved over time—more calories and calcium are needed to keep up with larger bodies and larger, more frequent eggs—we couldn't stray too far from the ancestral diet without fundamentally sacrificing the health of the birds (not to mention that of the eggs they produced). In other words: a bird cannot live on corn alone. And I'd rather not push the boundaries, either.

We'd been canning tomatoes, dilly beans, and cucumber pickles. Surely there had to be a way of preserving this corn for the long winter ahead. I thought about popcorn on the cob, multicolored ornamental corn, and the hard yellow ears sold in the local feed store to entertain and treat pet rodents. But in all my years of shopping at the grocery store, I'd never seen a corn pickle. I surmised that when it came to large-scale corn preservation, drying must be the tried-and-true route.

Unfortunately, there's not too much information about corn preservation online. Really, what American in her right mind would grow corn at all, let alone grow it and eschew the joy of eating it fresh, and instead turn it into an unappetizing shriveled cob of chicken food? But absurdity and lack of knowledge had never fazed us. How hard could it be to dry a few ears of corn?

. . . .

As it turns out, once it's pulled from the plant—a corncob left on the stalk, given warm and dry weather, will desiccate neatly inside the husk—the task of drying corn is very difficult indeed. We shucked hundreds of ears, a process that, I promise, is far more time consuming than you'd ever think possible. We placed them on newspapers in the backyard, and left the sun to do the work.

Within a week, the first batch sprouted fuzzy blue-gray mold. We realized that we couldn't leave the corn out overnight, because the Healdsburgian fog comes in on little cat feet and pees on our cobs, wetting them just enough to provide a nice damp environment for mildew.

So we altered our plan: ferry the corn out to the backyard in the morning and back into the house at night. The second batch fared better. For a while, it seemed like our corn was not grown in vain. Dubbing the cobs a success, we placed them in plastic bags and put them in the garage.

Where they promptly molded.

Well, you know what they say about the third time. Corn out during the day, in at night. We let this one dry even more thoroughly—the last batch we had left ever so slightly soft—and figured we could rehydrate it for the chickens later. And, we decided to forego plastic bags and instead use paper bags so that the dried corn could breathe.

Did I say paper bags? I should have used the singular: the leftover efforts of hundreds of corn plants could fit easily into one paper bag. Untold hours of effort yielded what felt like just a few ounces of dried corn, fit only for chickens.

. . . .

Corn is a grass. Ten thousand years ago, it was utterly unrecognizable from the huge cobs festooned with sweet, plump kernels we enjoy today. Corn comes from the wild, weedy Mexican grass called teosinte. Teosinte has an edible, nutritive seedpod that measures approximately four centimeters and possesses maybe six kernels, all in a single row. Picture an overgrown, unmowed lawn that has gone to seed and started taking steroids, and you have an approximate depiction of teosinte, with approximately the same stem-to-seed ratio. Lots of plant: little itty-bitty seeds.

It took thousands of years of artificial selection to turn that piddling 6-kernel cob into the 1,200-kernel monster corn is today. Along the way, *Zea mays* has been cultivated into specialized varieties: flour corn, sweet corn, popcorn, dent corn (primarily used for animal feed), ornamental corn, corncob corn (raised for the cobs, which transform into a solvent for extracting crude petroleum), high-lysine corn, and high-oil corn. Flavors of the eating ears range from sweet to starchy— but up until the 1950s, even the sweetest eating corn would start to lose its flavor shortly after harvest because the plant immediately began to convert the sugar into starch. For a long time, this is what kept people growing their own corn—and why local farmers bothered to grow it, too. Corn couldn't be kept longer than a day or two without losing its sweetness, and it couldn't be canned without adding loads of sugar and salt.

In the 1950s, the fate of the world's crops was still largely in the hands of farmers and agriculture universities. John Laughnan, a professor at the University of Illinois, published a paper in 1953 that he thought could be of use to the commercial corn industry: he'd devised a corn hybrid that contained four to ten times more sugar than the traditional sweet corn and, even more important, didn't convert that sugar into starch. He called it "supersweet."[41]

If there's one thing that college taught me, it's that scientists generally suck at communicating with the general public. Laughnan's supersweet corn—which had the potential to revolutionize the corn industry—flopped. It wasn't until the 1980s that seed companies got serious about developing commercially viable forms of this hybrid, and the agriculture world caught on to the potential brilliance of this concept. Now, corn can stay sweet for a week—plenty of time to get it from a field in Iowa to a grocery store in California and onto your plate. Americans produce 2.8 billion pounds of supersweet corn per year.[42] Yet that's just a drop in the bucket compared to the stuff we're growing for animals. Field corn—or corn destined to be processed and fed to cattle, hogs, or chickens— makes up the majority of the corn market. (My chickens are eating some of this corn in their grain ration.) In 2009, while all the country's farmers planted around 656,000 acres of sweet corn,[43] Mississippi alone planted 730,000 acres of field corn. And Mississippi isn't even among the top fifteen field corn– producing states. Feed grade corn covers eighty-five million acres nationwide; for every one acre of human corn, there are more than one hundred acres of livestock corn.

Ironically, American corn-fed cows would probably be better off if they were turned loose in a corn field to feast on the corn leaves and stalks. It is, after all, a grass. Instead, giant machines flatten the cellulose-rich corn stalks into the ground, strip them of their paltry two-per-stalk cobs, and feed *that* to the cattle that live thousands of miles away.

. . . .

Emmett's parents used to own livestock, but now they borrow them. In early summer—when the grasses on the property are as high as an elephant's knee, if not its eye—a motley herd arrived on the ranch. A friendly Brahman with huge wattles and a fleshy backpack, a couple of mean-looking bulls with their famously large heads, and a host of nervous new mamas and leggy calves ranged the property. They'd trim the grasses down to nubs, reducing the fire danger and fertilizing the ground for the following year's growth.

When our first planting of corn was harvested, Emmett's dad suggested that we feed the still-green corn stalks to the cows. We piled them up in a pickup truck and, feeling a bit like we were in a car commercial, drove it out on the range.

You know how cows have a tendency to look dumb and bored? So dumb you almost don't feel guilty when you start a car guessing game of how many hamburgers would that black and white one make?

Well, the free-range cows on the property did not look stupid. They looked rabid.

As soon as they spotted the heap of corn stalks spilling over our tailgate, they barreled down the hill toward the truck, lowing urgently. Emmett quickly climbed into the truck bed and I remained in the driver's seat; he tossed corn stalks out the back while I kept the truck moving so we wouldn't be entirely surrounded by several tons of overly enthusiastic ruminants. Still, a couple of the cows had clearly decided that the stalks in the truck were always better than the stalks on the ground. While the rest of the herd was content to munch on the stalks we'd tossed them, five cows doggedly pursued the pickup, easily extending their heads over the truck's side to munch on the stalk pile.

After a while, Emmett and I traded places so I could experience the adrenaline rush of jumping into the middle of a cow feeding frenzy. Perched on top of a pile of corn stalks, wobbling as the truck lumbered over bumps, I was knocked over by the huge head of an animal trying to wrest food from me before I even had the chance to toss it overboard. I'd always wanted to go on safari: maybe this was it. *Over to our left, a black-backed jackal feasts on a dik-dik gazelle. Look! A giraffe and her calf lumbering up to our truck. Now, watch out for the rhinos . . .*

they know we have food in the truck, and they can be quite aggressive when they're hungry. . . .

And then the thought occurred to me: at our farm, corn wasn't a subsistence crop, or even a cash crop. It would never be perfect, and we needn't expect it to be: let the corn worms eat a little cake, and the ants eat a little corn worm. From now on I'd measure the worth of corn not by the number of ears it produced or the dollars it brought in, but by the excitement of those it fed. I thought back to the faces that lit up at the farmers' market, drawn in to our stand to make other purchases; the chickens that played tag with the corn worms for hours; the cows that raced for a taste of green grass in the middle of the brown California summer and, in their eagerness, bowled over their hapless feeder.

Maybe corn wasn't so useless after all—assuming that you used the entire plant and that you were able to find at least a few worm friendlies in your community. And somehow corn seemed more elegant when approached holistically: kernels for humans, who bred them over the years to satisfy our need for quick calories; stalks for cattle, who had been eating similar grasses for most of history; and worms for the chickens, whose close cousins still subsist almost solely on bugs and grubs.

And who, at ten weeks old, were entirely capable of snatching and safely digesting even the fattest, meanest, king-pin corn worm—much to the delight of a certain worm-hating chicken keeper.

Chapter 8:

THE LONG WAIT

··

Winter Squash

In mid-October on a market morning, dawn didn't arrive at the field until 7:00 a.m.—about the same time we did. I pulled my station wagon up next to the compost pile. Emmett was already unloading harvest bins from the pickup. His breath puffed white, and beyond him, stripes of silver anointed the ground.

I scrambled out of the car, pulling down my wool hat and tugging my scarf a bit tighter.

"Did you *see* this?" I asked Emmett, who'd arrived a few minutes before me.

"I know, isn't it gorgeous?"

Frost coated the wide green leaves of each winter squash plant, catching and tossing back tiny pieces of the early morning light. In the furrows of the newly planted winter garden, frost highlighted the trench walls, tracing the contours of soil matter, the compost and bits of leaves, the rough manure and smooth chunks of clay.

We had harvesting to do and a market to get to, but still we stole a few minutes for wonder.

"Look at this!" I said. "The hose is frozen; I can't water." In San Diego, hoses never freeze, and somehow the fact that this one was frozen made me giggle.

We both wandered around for a few minutes, breathing in the sharp air, blinking the cold away from our eyeballs, examining different parts of the transformed field. And then I noticed something.

"Hey, Emmett," I called out. "I think the winter squash has frostbite."

On each beige butternut squash, a darker color splashed across the top of the gourd. I checked the delicata: same thing. Ditto for the spaghetti, sweet dumpling, jack-o'-lanterns, and pie pumpkins. All appeared to have suffered some sort of frost damage.

"Did we just wreck our winter squash? I thought we were supposed to leave them out through the first frost." We'd heard that we were supposed to wait for the first freeze to kill off the winter squash plants: it would be easier to pick out the gourds, and it sweetened them up, too.

"I don't know," Emmett replied. "But there's not much we can do about it now."

"Hmmm," I said. "I guess this means the end of the cucumbers, zucchini, and crookneck squash."

The thought dampened my mood a bit, but it didn't bring negativity so much as a sense of solemnity. Ecclesiastes, right? And that song by The Byrds?

It occurred to me that there aren't just four seasons—there are thousands. And the season we were in right then lasted only one morning. The world was as white as it would ever be in coastal California. The planet's finest lace—spiderwebs hung with frozen drops—overlaid iridescent green gowns. There was no end here; just possibility. After all, I couldn't water, the dark garden hose was stiff and frozen.

. . . .

We had planted the squash three and a half months earlier. As far as I could tell, the intervening weeks comprised something of a miracle, or maybe a series of miracles.

As we set about planning our squash field, Emmett's dad described a longtime Italian friend who planted winter squash without watering them at all. This man knew precisely the time of the season when the ground would still be wet enough to trigger the seeds' germination, and the air sufficiently warmed to ensure that the frost wouldn't sweep in and burn the seedlings. He'd stick the seeds in the ground and, *ecco*, they'd sprout

A winter squash swelled throughout the summer before ripening and changing color.

without any irrigation. In the clay soil of a river's floodplain, overhead watering forms a crust that can be difficult for tender seedlings to break through—so his was a valuable skill indeed.

Italian legends. French, Italian, Japanese, and American squash. And it was a Mexican man who taught us how to plant them all.

I don't speak Spanish and couldn't catch the few words I did know from the man who had spoken it for sixty years. Enrique mimed with some exaggeration for me, and talked to Emmett, who translated. Dig a hole. Fill it with water. Wait. Maybe an afternoon, maybe a day, maybe two or three days. When it's reached the perfect moisture level—he poked his finger in the side of the hole—where it's easy to push the seed in, but not so soupy as to cause the seed to rot before it reaches the surface, stick four seeds in the side of the wall. East, west, north, south. Fill in the hole with moist dirt, then compact the soil by pushing a fist down onto it or walking on top of it, then sprinkle dry dirt on the top.*

And then wait.

Miraculously, without any additional water, Enrique told us, in about a week the seedlings would start poking through the dry dust. The surface they sprouted from may look like a desert, but their roots would be firmly fixed in the moist soil beneath.

We planted 11 rows with 25 mounds apiece, 3 or 4 plants per mound: 825 plants. Jack-o'-lantern, Marina di Chioggia, spaghetti, sugar pie, Sibley, baby Hubbard, delicata, sweet dumpling, kuri, acorn, kabocha, and Long Island cheese.

And before we knew it, the field was littered with tiny green things. Winter squash seedlings are like beans: robust

---

*The compacted soil holds the moisture in and the loose, dry soil prevents a hard crust from forming on top. Some call the powdery cover a "dust mulch."

and ready for action from the start. After they broke the surface, they rapidly unfurled three good-sized leaves. Then we weeded them for the first and last time. Later on, we'd hoe the paths for ease of walking, but these plants would shade out most competitors in short order.

Overnight (or so it seemed) they sprawled along the ground and wasted little time with courtship. The first male blossoms—showy, bright orange, the size of my hand—were rapidly followed by female blossoms, equally showy and possessed of a small, hard, round green fruit.

With the arrival of the first few flowers, we panicked. Where were the bees? We had no problem attracting flea beetles and cucumber beetles to dine on the tender young leaves of our brassicas. But here we were offering what were clearly the world's finest flowers, and no bees bothered to show up for supper.

We had heard of a supposed solution to lack of bees: hand pollination. In China, this is a way of life. In some areas of the country, all apple trees are pollinated by the hands of farmers. Worried that our crop wouldn't set fruit, Emmett and I personally attended to the first adolescent bushes. We plucked out the male stamens and pressed them into the female flowers, smashing them together awkwardly.

Bees are gentler as they perform the act of entomophily. They slip inside the petals and sip on sugary nectar, filling their honey stomachs. Yellow dust coats their furry abdomens and clings to the hairs on their legs. They groom themselves, concentrating the protein-rich pollen into pollen sacs behind the bees' knees to bring back to the hive. Thus costumed in the flower's sperm, and all the while processing the nectar into honey, they head to the next flower, where they repeat the process. Yellow dust shakes from the bee's torso and fertilizes the pistil. New pollen commingles with the old, coating the bee further. The bee *is* the act of flower sex: at once delicate, sloppy, and sensual.

And then there was Emmett and me, feeling rather sordid as we tore out the male parts of the flowers and forced them against the female parts. It wasn't a job I enjoyed, and considering the size of the field, it could take days, or even weeks, to pollinate all of the squash. I thought of the recent spate of emptied hives, victims of Colony Collapse Disorder. The work performed by insect pollinators is truly unparalleled, and estimated to be worth $57 billion per year in the United States.[44] Humans have been able to mechanize almost every aspect of the growing process in order to mass produce food— but so far we haven't found a replacement for bees, and if we don't ensure their continued survival, we'll soon find ourselves spending untold hours raping flowers.

Fortunately, our luck soon changed. The presence of bees tends to be proportional to the presence of flowers, and it seemed that there was a minimum number of flowers required to attract their attention in the first place. Once our flowers became an unstoppable force—flamboyant orange diner signs littering a green freeway—the bees came. And so did the opportunity for an early harvest from our winter squash vines.

With the flowers out in droves, I'd zip around the field on market mornings chasing the bees, trying (like them) to find the biggest and brightest flowers. I'd snip them with florist shears and carefully place each blossom on a cookie sheet, which, when full, would in turn be placed in the most pampered spot in the truck: my lap. On our inaugural flower harvest, a disoriented bee came careening out of the flower tray as we started down the road to market. First one, then another, and another, until the cab was buzzing with involuntary stowaways. They'd gone in for a morning swig of nectar and come out to find themselves in a whole new world. We escorted them out of the car windows, knowing that they'd never find their way back to the hive and sad to see them die.

At the market, the display of flaming orange flowers drew gasps from the customers, and even from other farmers. They'd be snatched up for fifty cents each, destined to be stuffed with feta or ricotta, folded into crepes or pancakes, or breaded and deep-fried. But eventually, the flower harvest slowed and we all but forgot about the winter squash. Emmett would turn on overhead sprinklers to water the jungle every few weeks—the squash field being the only part of our farm without drip irrigation—but other than that, the squash field was a no-man's land. We were too busy beating back the cucumbers, beans, summer squash, and tomatoes. Too busy canning tomatoes and trying to dry wormy corn. We didn't really remember the squash until September.

. . . .

At the farmers' market on the day of the first frost, we checked in with the other farmers. They chattered with each other: some had spotted frost on the side of the road on the way into town, but their fields were safe.

You could call it bad luck, but there's a reason that this season was ours alone. At night, heat radiates quickly from the earth. The air quietly rearranges itself, densest layers down. With a good arm and a miraculous parting of trees, you could throw a stone from our field and hit the Russian River. I imagine the cold air flowing like the waters, always seeking the low point, pressed down with the weight of an atmosphere that stretches 430 miles above it. The river channel is a pathway for so much: fog when it exists, cold air when it doesn't; salmon preparing to run and raccoons and deer and wild boar who root along its riverbanks. But it's the sunken air, not the salmon starting to move, that gives us our singular season. The coldest air for miles around settles on our field, chilling and killing the squash and the beans.

· ·

In September, we were startled. I was thinning beet seedlings, casting baby plants onto the path to die so that their neighbors could grow in stronger and faster, when Emmett called me out to the squash field.

There, on the corner by the dirt road, rested a huge orange pumpkin. How something so obvious could have snuck up on us was beyond my comprehension.

We wandered the field, which was suddenly filled with almost-pumpkins, almost-butternuts, almost-spaghettis. Everything the size it ought to be, but green. A few of the early

The bounty of fall: squashes, pumpkins, and melons.

ripeners had turned their proper colors: bright orange, beige, daffodil yellow. There were petite and perfect sweet dumplings and dark green turban-shaped monsters. (Lost in the dozen varieties we planted, we'd tell customers they were ornamental and sell them cheaply, until we suddenly remembered that those monsters were actually Marina di Chioggia, a sought-after heirloom Italian squash that's delectable in ravioli and risotto.)

Some plants—tomatoes, zucchini, cucumbers, beans—spend their energy pumping out fruit after fruit, taking the scattershot approach to spreading their seed. But these winter squash plants had taken an entire season to produce just a few vehicles for the next generation. One monstrous plant; two, maybe three, pumpkins.

. . . .

At the market, Emmett and I packed up the leftover cucumbers and summer squash for the last time this year. Other farmers would continue to carry these relics of summer for the next few weeks, but not us.

When we got back to the field, every member of the cucurbit family was toast, the morning's silvery scene replaced by a despondent field filled with brown, collapsed vines. It was as though a fire had swept through and left behind femurs of forest, house ribcages—a miniature version of familiar Southern California firestorms without the ash rain.

Freezing isn't unlike burning. As water crystallizes, it expands: hydrogen bonds straighten out and lock into place. The individual cells of plants are comprised primarily of water. When they freeze, their rigid walls shatter. When they melt, the thawed, life-giving water leaks uselessly out of the broken cell—evaporating into a gas, which is just what happens in a fire.

And as it turns out, experts agree that you're supposed to harvest winter squash *before* the first frost; the bit about ease of harvesting is true, but with the usual catch-22 of any old wives' tale. Specifically, while the gourds are easier to pick out in the field, they don't keep as well if they've been frosted.

Not wanting to leave them out for another night, we gathered our weapons. Confronted with buck knives and pruning shears, the fruits easily dissevered from the vines. We placed them in piles by type and ferried armfuls to the back of the truck. A quarter of the field filled the pickup's long bed and heaped high over the rails.

So much of the farmers' market is about summer. Bright, bold fruits and flavors—color and crunch and panache. We'd earn less now that these sexy moneymakers were gone, but somehow I was okay with the trade. It's fine to revel in the bounty when you have it, but revelry doesn't get you through the winter. Storage does.

And right now, we had three pickup beds' worth of winter squash to get us through the winter. Round, oblong, short, and squat, they'd join their cousins to keep us fed until spring rolled around again. The tomatoes had been skinned, deflated, boiled, acidified, and crammed into a jar. The cucumbers and beans, ensconced in apple cider vinegar and garlic, were discolored and softened. The potatoes—which under perfect conditions could keep for months—would soon start to sprout, sending long, skinny tendrils out of wooden boxes in the basement.

But the last miracle was this: Without any preservation effort on my part, frost damage and all, the squash would keep through winter, spring, and summer, well into the following fall.

Chapter 9

BUM NUTS

· ·

And Other Chicken Firsts

As soon as I saw Hope in the coop, I knew what it meant. I walked purposefully back to the house and opened the front door.

"Emmett!" I shouted without entering. "I think Hope's about to lay an egg!" I slammed the door shut and sprinted back to watch.

My chickens wouldn't be caught dead in the coop during the day. As soon as I'd open the doors in the morning, they would fly out—an exodus of feathers, pine shavings, and dust—and spend the day roaming the pasture. They entered the coop only if they were craving a midday grain snack, or when it was nearing sunset and time to lay claim to the best sleeping spots.

It was winter, and the sun was low enough in the sky that direct light shone through the old, southern-facing window we had framed into the coop for this very reason. Although the glass was dirty, the light that shone through was crisp. And there Hope stood, in the coop in broad daylight, framed by clean light slanting through the dusty window. It was as though she was caught in the spotlight, and even her shadow was nervous about it. She had a bee in her bonnet—and, I was wagering, an egg up her bum.

I picked her up and placed her in one of our newly minted nest boxes. She settled right in. After a few minutes, she got up, perched on the edge of the box, and peered down at the nest as though wondering whether it was a worthy spot for whatever grand occasion was about to take place. A Rhode Island Red hopped up and cocked her head, one eye squarely facing Hope: whatcha doin'? With that, Hope settled back into the nest, fluffing her feathers and flattening her body into a position I'd not seen her assume before. When I nudged in for a closer look, she raised her feathers like hackles and emitted a draconic roar. I decided that, given the circumstances, permitting her some privacy was appropriate.

If you haven't raised chickens, this probably seems like much ado about nothing. After all, every schoolchild knows that chickens lay eggs: it's what they've been bred for seven thousand years to do and why I brought them into my home in the first place. But those who share my poultry addiction will understand the intense anticipation. I had waited six months for this moment—no, I'd *worked* six months for this moment, from the first slice of the saw through a two-by-four to form the skeleton for the first failed chicken coop, to the weeks spent constructing the second Fort Knox, to the hours spent feeding, cleaning, caretaking, and generally obsessing over my brood. Not to mention the hundreds of pounds of organic chicken feed I'd gone through to reach this moment. (Another author spoke of a $64 tomato, and I refused to actually perform the math on my eggs so as not to vindicate Emmett's skepticism about my fledgling chicken business. Still, I can safely say that between the coops and feed, this would be somewhere in the ballpark of a $1,000 egg. In my defense, my chickens would earn around $100 a week after they hit full production.)

In a couple of hours, Hope had disappeared from the coop and nest, and in her place sat a tiny, sky-blue egg. It was so small, in fact, that after we brought it into the house for safe-keeping, we couldn't quite figure out how to display it best. We tried showcasing it in an eggcup, but it settled down into the hollow, not even protruding above the ceramic surface. Placed in a basket, the egg looked laughably lonely. And still I couldn't stop admiring it. It was five months' worth of hope, after all.

....

Our new layer didn't miss a beat. She cranked out tiny blue eggs every day. After we'd amassed four, although they probably added up to only one grocery store extra-large, we figured it was close enough to a meal. We fried them and ate them on toast with an air of ceremony. They may have been small, we noted, but they packed a punch: they stood up pertly in the pan, and when we forked into the yolks and they bled out onto the bread, the color was a brilliant orange tending toward red. And they would get bigger with time, too. Pullets (young hens) start out laying small eggs, but as they mature, their eggs creep up in size until they resemble those from the grocery store.

In another week, a second Ameraucana joined Hope in the nest boxes, and soon we found ourselves gifted with two eggs nearly every day. Then a Rhode Island Red came into production, adding brown shells to our colorful collection. Perhaps incensed by her new competition, Hope found a way to out-do them: she started on an every-other-day double-yolker schedule. Double yolkers are the avian equivalent of mammalian

One of our first double-yolk eggs towered over its single-yolk counterparts.

twins—but because the logistics of breaking out of an egg are considerably different from those of giving birth, these eggs would never hatch naturally. There simply wouldn't be enough room for both birds to fight their way into the world. Double yolkers don't make it in the commercial food world, either: grocery stores hinge on standardization and packaging. They're too tall to fit in standard cartons, so the simple pleasure of cracking open an oversized egg and finding two yolks is one known to backyard keepers alone. And although there are plenty of arguments to be made against keeping chickens—they're dirty, they eat everything in sight, they tie you down, they're prone to dying just as soon as they grow on you—it's the double yolkers and the delight of gathering still-warm eggs from a straw nest that make it worthwhile.

And at first, I was oddly hesitant to share these joys. Intellectually I knew that the chickens would keep laying—we were now past the solstice and as the days grew longer, they'd only produce more—but still, I had a hard time trusting that they would. I fought the urge to hoard my golden eggs. It hadn't quite hit me that, like the responsibilities, the gifts of the chicken are a daily act.

"We'll keep getting more," Emmett told me, after I expressed regret that he sold a precious dozen to one of our farmers' market customers, who made a special trip out to our farm to pick them up.

The man had never spoken truer words.

. . . .

I had a theory: if twenty-five chickens were fun, then fifty chickens must be twice the fun. I'd been assured by local egg sellers that although it wouldn't be twice the work—certain chores, like tucking the chickens in at night and letting them out in the morning, took a fixed amount of time—it would mean twice the number of eggs to sell.

I'd been ruminating on this theory for a couple of months. In those two months, diving deeper into the addiction, I'd become a bit of a (dare I say?) chicken snob. Right now, I only had *hatchery* birds—which, according to poultry fanciers and PETA (one of the few subjects on which they agree), is the equivalent of a puppy-mill purebred. These birds are often mass-produced in large warehouses without much individual attention given to the characteristics that count on a small farm: the number of eggs produced per year, the age at which the bird reaches maturity, its longevity, personality, feed consumption, and ability to forage.

Hatcheries commit other sins disavowed by poultry snobs. They often sell blue egg–laying birds as "Ameraucanas/ Araucanas," which is approximately the same as labeling a dog a Golden Retriever/Chihuahua and calling it a purebred. The birds they sell are often similar to Ameraucanas but don't meet the color standard for the breed. And they're nothing like the bizarre Araucana—a truncated, rumpless chicken with feather-covered fleshy protuberances sticking out of its cheeks. The Araucana is extremely rare, partly because the rumpless characteristic can be affiliated with a lethal gene, and many eggs fail to hatch at all.

The point being: my Ameraucanas, including Hope, were mutts. Don't get me wrong, I loved my mutts, but if I was really committed to heritage livestock and the promotion of small family farms—not to mention humane, small-scale raising of poultry—I couldn't source solely from hatcheries.

So I took the advice of my addiction-enabling online friends, and ordered purebred heritage eggs from farms across the country. Other chicken-fancying farmers collected the eggs from their heritage flocks, lovingly packed each egg individually in bubble wrap and newspaper, and then mailed them a thousand miles to California—where I unpacked them, placed them in an incubator, and began to wait.

For the first eighteen days, there were plenty of ways to keep busy. Fortunately, my incubator came with an automatic egg-turner so I didn't need to rotate the eggs three times a day. However, once a day (and sometimes more), I slipped a digital hygrometer into the warm, humid incubator and waited for the temperature and humidity to level out on the screen. The automatically controlled temperature always hovered around 100 degrees F. The humidity, however, was a manual job and would fluctuate wildly if I wasn't careful. I had to figure out just how large a puddle in the bottom of the incubator was required to maintain a constant 35 to 40 percent humidity—and of course, as the puddle evaporated, I had to add additional liquid. After much debate, I decided to use the "dry incuba-tion" method, which called for increasing the humidity in the room and using smaller puddles inside the incubator for a lower humidity. To Emmett's great amusement, I draped wet towels everywhere, and once a day I boiled a kettle of water and placed it, still steaming, near the incubator.

On day fourteen, I candled the eggs. A pretty verb, to be sure, but more accurately I headlamped them. With a proper setup, you can actually see the embryo moving inside the egg. Since mine was primitive (me and an LED headlamp in a darkened room), I saw one of two things: a translucent egg, or one whose embryo was sufficiently developed to block some of the light. I left the translucent eggs in the incubator for a few days more, just to be safe, and after headlamping them a sec-ond time on day eighteen, I removed the blanks.

On day eighteen, I was supposed to increase the humidity substantially and—perhaps the most difficult direction of all to follow—*not open the incubator again until all the chicks were finished hatching.*

According to my obsessive-compulsive research, this could be a long process. Sometimes a chick breaks the shell—the first little tapped-out hole is called a "pip"—and then waits twenty-four hours before undertaking the second part of the hatching process. During this time, the nervous human mother hovering over the glowing incubator worries that the baby has died. She frets, she fidgets, but she must not open the incubator—losing humidity at this crucial step could be fatal to chicks still in the shell.

The second step in the hatching process is called zipping, for good reason. Baby birds are very careful. After a chick pips, it waits until it's absorbed the last of the yolk—until the blood vessels that have connected it to its life support system for the last three weeks have all dried down. If the chick hatches before this happens, it can literally bleed to death. But once it's ready for the world, it begins methodically tapping out a line of latitude around the egg. Its little egg-tooth (a sharpened point on the beak that falls off shortly after hatching) breaks through the eggshell while a lack of oxygen triggers the bird to kick, which helps it rotate neatly around the egg.

The trouble is, if you're using an artificial incubator, you might not have the humidity quite right. If it's too humid, the chick can literally drown. Over the course of the twenty-one-day incubation period, approximately 15 percent of the egg's water content must evaporate so that when the chick pips, it pips into an air cell—something that enables it to breathe just enough until it manages to break out into the greater atmosphere.

If the environment is too dry, however, the chick can get stuck inside the shell. The membrane that lines the calcareous shell is soft and supple when damp, but dries into something like glue.

Inside the Styrofoam walls of the incubator, a life and death drama waited to play out. The beauty is, chicks have been successfully hatching from eggs for thousands of years; life usually triumphs.

It was three o'clock in the morning when I was awakened by a shrill, angry cheeping coming from the incubator room. Not wanting to wake Emmett, I left the lights off and slipped into the incubator room to huddle over its red glow. One egg had been neatly broken in half, and on the wire mesh floor beside it, a tiny wet creature was heaving—and screaming its tiny little head off. After it screamed for a few seconds, it contorted, kicking out its feet and legs and head erratically, and convulsed across the floor. Once the chick stopped, it started cheeping again as if to say, "All that work for *this?*"

I couldn't stop the grin from spreading across my face. Watching baby chicks make their way into the world was like Christmas morning. Where for three weeks there was a wrapped package, beautiful and whole, suddenly there were ribbons and wrapping paper everywhere—and a brand-new life rolling around the floor.

I tore my eyes away from the angry little yellow thing to check the progress of the other eggs. Another chick was working its way out, and had zipped a quarter of the way around its egg. A third had broken out a little hole; its beak rested in the microscopic window, moving ever so slightly as it breathed.

I wished them luck, and slipped back into bed.

. . . .

Twenty-four hours later, puffy chicks in black and dark gray and reddish-yellow and silver were careening around the incubator, bumping into one another in their attempt to find nonexistent breakfast. And that little beak was still there. I'd been checking on it, waiting for it to make progress; a few times I saw it moving in and out like a saw, but it seemed unable to go anywhere. It had been in the same position for twenty-four hours, the allotted time period for the second phase of hatching.

I was pretty sure that the chick was stuck.

Now, some chicken fanciers believe that chicks that get stuck are stuck for a reason—they're not strong enough, they wouldn't have hatched on their own, so it's better to let them die. And then there are those of us who are suckers for tiny creatures trapped in enclosed spaces, trying valiantly to make their way into the world. Call it compassion, call it claustro-phobia, but the thought of dying dark and alone, tiny limbs trapped and intertwined, was too much for me to stomach.

There were still a couple of eggs that hadn't hatched; the "do not open" rule was still in effect. So I didn't *exactly* open the incubator. I draped it in hot, wet towels; Emmett cracked the lid open the tiniest bit; I slipped my hand under the tow-els and grabbed the egg. At the ready was a hastily assembled chick birthing kit: tweezers, a few Q-tips, a bowl of hot water, and paper towels. Wielding tweezers and mimicking the zip-ping step, Emmett flaked off bits of the egg around its equator while I moistened the membrane beneath with a Q-tip. We turned on a heat lamp and cradled the egg beneath it so the tiny creature inside wouldn't die of chill.

After Emmett had completed his circumnavigation of the egg, we waited. At this point, the chicken message boards told us, the chick should be able to give a swift kick and finish the job, splitting the egg in two and making its grand entrance into the world.

Nothing happened. The bird wiggled a bit, a tiny move-ment visible beneath the white membrane. All of our energy was focused on this tiny creature, willing it to kick off the shell.

Nothing happened. "Well," I said, "Let's keep going." Emmett continued to flake off bits of eggshell. I started to pull back the membrane. We looked anxiously for blood—there was none. We were safe.

After another minute, I decided it was time to get drastic. This had taken ten minutes, and despite the heat lamp, the egg was cooling to the touch. I pulled off the top half of the egg, and immediately saw why the chick was so attached to his little window. A part of the membrane had dried on to his forehead like cement, completely covering his eye. Emmett pulled off the wet membrane covering the chick's back and neck. Wetting the hardened part with a Q-tip, I winced as I slowly, steadily pulled it off, hoping that the eyelid wouldn't come with it. It didn't. Then I gently tipped up the bottom half of the egg.

A baby bird fell out into my hand and immediately commenced the psycho spaz dance performed by the other newly hatched chicks. Still curved into an egg shape, he was a skinny thing with slicked down feathers that looked like molten silver—a Splash Orpington, who when fully grown would be a huge, striking white bird flecked with gray. "Ready?" I asked Emmett. He nodded, and cracked open the incubator lid. I slipped the baby chick into a corner, away from his puffy brethren, so he could learn what it was like to move around in his own space without getting too trampled. Approximately one hour of rolling around the incubator seemed to straighten them out—but until then, everything about this tiny life was a prostrate curved comma, including its perfect, tiny feet.

. . . .

Salmon Faverolles are an exceptional chicken breed originating in France. The hens are sweet, good-natured beige ladies with feathered feet and puffy cheeks and chins. They possess five toes, rather than the typical four: a circus sideshow touch that compliments their whiskers and beards. They lay almost an egg a day all summer long—a tinted, cream-colored egg, the likes of which you'd never find in a grocery store—and enjoy foraging for weeds, bugs, and garden scraps.

The males are spectacular. They're built like tanks with low, heavy breasts, and wear plumage straight out of Chaucer. They have beards like a woodsman, dark and full. Add to that a long, luscious, black stallion tail and a cream-colored saddle with accents of mahogany, and you can picture them crowing over pilgrims wending their way to Canterbury.

Unlike other roosters, the Salmon Faverolle roosters are a completely different color than the females, yet another anomaly in the chicken world. It makes them easy to sex as youngsters: as their primary feathers grow in and replace the soft baby down, which happens about a week after hatching, you can easily tell the boys from the girls. This is exciting, because an untrained eye usually can't determine the sex of chickens for at least two months. And of course, everyone hopes to hatch out more pullets (proto-hens) than cockerels (proto-roosters).

I had put ten Salmon Faverolle eggs in the incubator. Cost of one dozen fertile eggs: $30. Cost of shipping them from a friendly farmer in Texas: $15. Cost of incubator: $120 (although I managed to con one out of my mother as a Christmas present). Cost of electricity required to keep incubator running for twenty-one days straight: at least $15.

Given my initial investment, I anxiously awaited the moment when I could officially determine the sex ratio of my clutch. I looked at pictures online; I picked the chicks up to hold their feathers up to the light. And each time I did, I thought, *Please tell me you're light brown, and not black.*

After two weeks, there was no denying it. Of my first Salmon Faverolle hatch, six out of eight chicks were male. To add insult to injury, one of the two females was a "sport" (a genetic anomaly)—white-colored instead of salmon. She'd make a fine egg-layer, but if I was trying to keep to the heritage breed standard, hers weren't the genetics that I'd want to pass along to the next generation.

What was there to do, besides go back to the drawing board and order more eggs? And since my incubator held forty

The surviving seven chickens perched in the small coop.
(Hope is second from the left.)

eggs, why not fill it up? I contacted farms and ordered some Salmon Faverolles, Blue Orpingtons, and Buff Orpingtons, and fired up the incubator again.

....

Cockerels, like all young animals, are cute. Roosters, however, are not. In fact, they're parasites. If you retain all of your cockerels and permit them the luxury of turning into roosters, the first thing that will happen is your feed bill will go through the roof and your egg business might not even break even. The second thing that will happen—unless you build an entirely separate coop and yard for the boys, which again is cost prohibitive—is that your hens will be miserable.

As soon as they mature, roosters turn into hungry, noisy, horny, sexually deviant motherfuckers. They will pick out an individual hen and chase her around the coop, yard, pasture, driveway, and porch until eventually she tires enough to be mounted. They will also gang-rape hens; five or six roosters will chase down a hen together and form a ring around her. After one rooster mounts her, everyone else has to have their way with her, too. During this whole process, the hen—as you'd might expect—is screaming her head off and frantically trying to get away. But she can't, because she's surrounded on every side by more horny roosters.

As if that weren't bad enough, when they mount the hen, the roosters bite the feathers on the back of her head and dig their talons into her back. After only a few weeks of rooster-fest, my hens were sporting bare backs and bald spots. They no longer looked like happily free-ranging beauties, but abused factory-farmed critters.

I grew up in a household that eschewed Barbie for her unrealistic, over-sexualized view of the female form. To me, the meaning of roosterfest was clear: patriarchy had set up shop in my chicken pasture. Remember, the gentle hens are the ones who do all the work, passing an egg that comprises 3 percent of their body weight every twenty-six hours. Scaling up, this is the equivalent of a 150-pound woman giving birth to a 5-pound baby every day. Meanwhile, the roosters eat, sleep, shit, crow, fight, and fuck. And all of these processes are repeated at least a dozen times in the course of twenty-four hours.

My rooster-dominated yard was cruel. It was embarrassing when visitors stopped by to see the happy free-range chickens—and instead found themselves explaining to their kids what the roosters were violently doing to the hens. The roosters were inhaling chicken feed, too; a fifty-pound bag disappeared every other day. It had to stop.

I admit, roosters are quite beautiful. And in order to breed heritage chickens I'd need to keep a few of them. But empathy for my hens overcame my general animal empathy, and I realized that an egg-eating vegetarian is essentially a chicken-eating vegetarian, anyway. If you eat eggs, male chickens somewhere are dying. (Ditto, by the way, for most male dairy animals.) With this realization, I'd just grasped a fundamental tenet of livestock management: female animals are useful; male animals are not. Or, more accurately, female animals are useful *alive* while male animals are not.

It would be fine if livestock were magically born in a 1:10 male-female ratio. But they're 1:1, just like the rest of us. (And with my luck, they're 2:1, with the males outweighing the females.) The truth is, you need only a few males to keep a large herd or flock of females going.

Most male chickens don't even get the chance at life: they're tossed by the hundreds into trashcans and left to suffocate. Male dairy cows, thin-boned and lightweight, aren't worth the feed to raise them into steers. They'll never have the steak-growing capacity of Anguses or Longhorns—stout breeds specifically developed for muscle mass. So male dairy cows are slaughtered young, and their anemic, weak flesh—which usually hasn't seen the light of day, much less an exercise yard—becomes veal parmigiana.

Emmett and I could choose to look the other way. We could sell our roosters to the local feed store, where someone less thin-skinned would pick them up for a few dollars and turn them into dinner. (Or worse—since there's a strong cockfighting culture in Sonoma County, the roosters could very well end up in the ring.) We could go on pretending that we were vegetarian, even though our desire for eggs—and our need to safeguard the hens who produced them—had signed the death warrant for male chickens under our care. Hell, we could tell ourselves that the animals were going to be picked up by another farmer who desperately wanted to provide a safe, happy home for roosters.

Fuck that.

Emmett got out the hatchet. And I went to get the Buff Chanticleer.*

I've heard it argued that the way a creature lives doesn't matter. That when he's facing the hatchet, whether it's in a huge processing plant or at the hands of the farmer who raised him, he's still going to fight like hell. He's still going to die a miserable death, he's still going to suffer, he's still going to do everything in his power to cling to life.

Later I'd have roosters that struggled. But I'm telling you, the Buff Chanticleer's attitude was so accommodating that it caused me to wonder whether I had a reincarnated Zen master on my hands—one who had screwed up and was patiently waiting for death so he could have another shot at personhood again.

Normally roosters hate being held. I simply walked up to the Chanticleer and scooped him up, where he waited sweetly in my arms, more like a lapdog than the testosterone-filled rapscallion that he was.

Emmett and I spent fifteen minutes postponing the inevitable, during which time the rooster didn't let out so much as a peep. We laid him down on the stump over and over, pressed his head this way and that, trying to determine what position would grant the cleanest, quickest death. He patiently bore our ministrations until we felt certain we had the best shot at a one-swing death.

---

*The Buff Chanticleer was another example of my knack for beating the sex-ratio odds: out of three "straight run" chicks I picked up from a local chicken fancier—which should have had about a 50:50 male-female ratio—I got all roosters.

I held him, and Emmett—with stronger muscles and surer aim—swung the freshly sharpened hatchet home.

． ．

Yes, the bird continued to spasm and flap after the head had been severed from its body. Yes, there was blood. But there wasn't much of it, and within fifteen minutes—after a ten-minute bleed-out period, a quick scald at 145 degrees F in a water bath, and some frantic feather plucking before the skin cooled down—we had something that didn't look like *a* chicken. Rather, it looked like chicken. Reaching this point was cause for celebration: the chicken was quite definitively dead, and stripped of the things (head, feathers) that made it look personable. We were no longer standing guiltily by a woodshed with a live bird and a hatchet, wondering whether one of the cyclists breezing by on the road would careen into a tree when he glanced up to see us hanging a flapping, headless chicken from the rafters. Now the chicken was not only dead, but also dead looking; no fingers were severed in the process, and the tears that were shed had since dried; no bicyclists came to harm, and as far as we knew, they had their eyes on the road and we were the only witnesses to the murder. Success, right?

Surely, we thought, the hard part was over. After this it should all be smooth sailing. Within minutes, we'd have an oven-ready bird, stuffed with halved lemons, garlic cloves, and rosemary sprigs, its supple skin rubbed with salt, pepper, and vegan butter, some sage leaves slid under the skin.

Ha.

Postpone that vision of a perfect oven-ready carcass for, oh, three more hours. In its place, picture two idiots with a blunt knife tentatively slicing into a bird's dead, naked ass. For an hour. Then picture a certain city slicker (chosen because her hand was significantly smaller than the country boy's) sticking her fingers into the aforementioned bird's ass. For another hour—during which she repeatedly smells her hand, which smells exactly like concentrated chicken shit. Only then, in the third hour, would the actual organs be removed.

We moved tentatively through the chicken cutting and gutting process, terrified of rupturing the gallbladder or the lower intestine, a mistake that would result in spoiled meat. After such a traumatic process (for us, not to mention the bird), we didn't want the bird's death to be in vain.

So, to be sure the meat stayed edible, we spent the next three hours trying to *gently* cut into the bird's cavity and *delicately* remove its organs. None of the websites we referenced, some of which contained very detailed, graphic pictures of the process, deigned to mention that all of the organs were suspended in connective tissue that resembled in strength and texture those giant spiderwebs that nearly frustrate Frodo and his friends in their ring quest. None of them mentioned that if you touched the bird's lower intestine, even if that intestine wasn't ruptured and the meat hadn't been spoiled, your hands would smell like concentrated chicken shit. And that an extremely sharp knife wasn't just handy: it was necessary. Also, that a substantial amount of courage would be required to stick your hand blindly into the rooster's still-warm viscera, even if that rooster was a rapist. And that even more courage would be required to plunge in, grab a fistful of viscera, and yank. HARD. Perhaps this should be obvious, but I for one would have appreciated being told that there is no room for gentleness when it comes to evisceration.

In other complications, all of the websites we referenced detailed the processing of Cornish Cross chickens, a hybrid bird specifically developed for meat production. Our hand-some heritage fellow was nothing like these birds. Cornish Crosses are, as far as I'm concerned, not real chickens. They're Frankenchickens. I'd encountered them a few times, most notably at an Amish farm in upstate New York, where they seemed woefully out of place with the bonneted children and hand-sewn laundry flapping in the breeze. The birds I saw were, at the tender age of two months, ready for slaughter. Heritage birds don't really flesh out until six months or so: our Buff Chanticleer was eight months old at the time of his death, having been purchased as a chick from a local chicken fancier shortly after our fox tragedy. The Cornish Crosses did not race around the pasture, chasing insects, flying up into trees, and clambering on top of the hens like my rooster did; rather, they walked a few steps and then lurched into a sitting position, exhausted by the effort required to carry the weight of their own breasts. All in all, they seemed dull, pathetic, and somehow revolting—even in the ideal, sustainable "chicken tractor" model that the Amish farmers were using. While the chickens were free-range, they never got further than a few feet from the tractor, so the term didn't seem to mean much. (And by the way, even the free-range, organic chickens from Whole Foods are Cornish Crosses.) These weren't chickens: these were pre-meats that happened to eat and breathe.

By contrast, our rooster was a living, breathing entity that happened to become meat. His smaller breast and body cavity meant it was harder to stick a hand inside him to get the organs out. His age also meant that he possessed some things that the two-month-olds lacked. More on this later.

Some aspects of processing heritage birds and Cornish Crosses are the same. Like step one: removing the feet. With a knife tip inserted in the joint, they snap off easily. Swallowing my disgust, I bucked up and processed the feet so that I could use them later to add richness to our chicken soup. I dipped them briefly in boiling water and then "pulled off the socks," which is an entirely pleasant euphemism for an entirely unpleasant procedure. Starting at the ankle, I removed, in one multi-toed sheet, the scaly skin covering the foot. A couple of toenails popped off in the process. I pulled off the other two that didn't, and then repeated the process for the other foot. Both "sockless" feet went into the refrigerator

Step two: removing the oil gland. This was another simple, outside-the-body step that involved cutting off a fatty section of the triangular tail that was said to give an off-flavor to the meat. It took a few slices, but eventually I removed all of the yellow fat on the tail.

Now the bad news: Everything up until this point was the easy part. Next, it was time to blindly cut into the bird's bum without cutting into its large intestine (which obviously terminates right there). After poking at the bird with a dull knife for fifteen minutes, we finally made a tiny, finger-sized hole. Another forty-five minutes of additional hacking, and a circle large enough to accommodate a very small human hand exposed the bird's cavity, filled with a confusing mess of grayish organ blobs.

Emmett made a chivalrous first attempt at sticking his hand in the cavity, but couldn't squeeze in more than a few fingers—no way were his broad knuckles fitting past the narrow hips.

"I'll do it!" The way I said it made it sound like I was volunteering out of the kindness of my heart, although clearly I was the only option left. I seemed to have fooled Emmett, though: he acted surprised by my generous offer.

"Are you sure?" he asked.

I acted offended by the question. "It's my rooster, isn't it?"

Brave face on, I plunged in . . . to the warm, squishy, what-the-fuck-am-I-doing-here land that comprises the innards of a chicken.

. . . .

We'd been taking turns trying to disembowel the rooster for forty-five minutes. I was able to stretch the cavity a bit, making it large enough so that Emmett could just barely jam his hand in. At the moment, he was the one wrist-deep in bird guts.

"Just pull!"

"I can't, I think something's breaking." He stared at the dead rooster, a look of concentration on his face, apparently trying something new with his fingers and the viscera. "It's all stuck in there, it won't budge."

"Well, can't you just grab and pull?"

"I'm trying! There's no room for me to open my hand."

"Obviously, people do this," I said. "So we should be able to. Here, let me try again."

I stuck my hand inside the bird—the slippery organs once again refused to be caught by my fingers—and wished for this to be over. We were getting snappy with each other, and even snappier when we thought about how many more roosters were still running around raping hens in the yard. (Twenty-one, to be exact.) We'd been at this for over two hours now—closer to three if you counted the catching, stressing, and killing part. At this rate, it would only take us seven nine-hour days to process all of our roosters.

My mind was elsewhere—counting chicken breeds and the number of roosters we'd need to keep—when suddenly I noticed that I was using my fingernails to slice through the connective tissue and loosen the organs from the walls. Which was gross, but I seemed to be making progress.

Emmett went to open a window. The smell of dead chicken was really starting to get to me. "You know, I really think we've broken the fucking intestine," I said. "It smells disgusting. How the hell are we supposed to eat this shit?" I pulled out my hand and thrust it in Emmett's nose. "Ugh, smell it."

"Don't shove your nasty fingers in my face!" he said, swerving away.

"I'm just saying, I think it's too late for this rooster. I think we wrecked it."

I pulled out my hands, walked over to the sink, ran painfully hot water over my fingers, and started scrubbing. Emmett reached into the rooster with a look of resolve that mirrored the look he had worn just before swinging the hatchet.

"Well, I may as well just yank everything out, then."

"Don't break it! We might not have ruined it yet. Be careful, would you?"

From my vantage point, I couldn't be sure what was happening inside the rooster, but clearly I had loosened the jar lid. Emmett's face was impassive as, with one pull, he brought a mass of organs out. He spotted the bright green gallbladder and separated it from the pile. A second pull brought the last of it out—heart, lungs, gizzard.

The lungs, spongy and pink, seemed to come out whole—at least, I couldn't see anything missing from them. But our chicken-processing guides warned us that they'd left behind plenty of lung tissue jammed between the chicken's ribs and suctioned on to the chest wall like glue. Apparently those who regularly eviscerate chickens have a special tool for the removal of lung tissue. Ever the resourceful vegetarians, we used a grapefruit spoon.

Once we scraped the lung tissue out with our serrated spoon, rinsed, and repeated, we were in a good place. The heart, gizzard (a muscular purse filled with dozens of tiny jewel-like stones), trachea, and lungs were removed. The dangerous bile-filled gallbladder was out, and the poop-filled intestine was loosened from the cavity and pulled safely outside the bird. To finish up, Emmett cut around the base of the intestine. "You realize what you're doing," I told Emmett. "You're literally ripping it a new one."

He didn't appreciate my humor, but after three hours of organ removal my soul screamed out for crass jokes and beer.

I had to fight the urge to whine, "Are we done?" The intestine and gallbladder were in a bucket ready to be thrown away. The rinsed heart, liver, and gizzard were in a Mason jar in the fridge with the feet. But just when we thought we'd finished, Emmett spotted another organ situated high inside the cavity—up in the chest, the part that the rooster sticks out proudly when he crows.

"What the hell is this?"

"Uh, liver? No, wait, there are two of them. Kidney?"

And then I noticed two skinny white tubes, attached to what I thought were the kidneys, going down to the animal's rear end.

"Jesus. I think those would be the testicles."

Ah, yes. Here was what those two-month-old Cornish Crosses lacked. No wonder my roosters were always so horny: their testes were literally the size of their hearts. I winced as I pulled them out and, in doing so, severed the tubes. A white liquid oozed out of them and into the body cavity. "Yum," I told Emmett, "Rooster jizz!"

And then I rinsed out the body cavity with cold running water seven times, just to be sure no rooster tadpoles ended up in my gravy. Exhausted, we placed the rooster in a cooler with ice to rest overnight and resolved to cook it the following day.

....

I grew up eating meat, but it had been about seven years since I'd cooked it myself. To roast the rooster, I had to reach back deep into the memory bank, which in my case was more of a memory colander. I have a knack for remembering stories, but I rarely hold on to the facts that accompany them. So I remembered the arc of the roast: the naked massage with butter, salt, and herbs, and the offerings—lemon, rosemary, garlic—stuffed inside the cavity; the frequent checking, basting, and temperature-taking; and the glorious finale when it's pulled out of the oven, sliced into, and presented flawlessly on a white platter.

But I had no idea how to get from naked massage to plated, browned bird. I called my mom to check what temperature I should set the oven for, and made up the rest.

My bird, which had plenty of food to eat but was also very active, had less fat than confined birds. I slipped a couple of spoonfuls of vegan butter under the skin, above the breast where it would melt and ooze down to soak the meat. I rubbed the outside with more vegan butter, and then rubbed salt and pepper onto that. After checking the Internet's opinion, I turned up the oven temperature to "seal in the flavors" for the first ten minutes before lowering it to my mother's suggested temperature. I rubbed the cavity with a mixture of salt, pepper, and chopped rosemary, then filled it with the bounty of our farm fields: halved Meyer lemons, four rosemary sprigs, several peeled garlic cloves, and a halved and peeled onion.

Into the oven went the bird.

As the fat leaked down into the glass pan, it started to burn. I added a little white wine to the bottom of the pan and basted the bird periodically with the wine/fat mixture. As the delicious smell of roast chicken filled the air, Emmett stuck a thermometer in the thigh to make sure it was safely cooked. It was, and he carved.

If hatching chicks were Christmas, then this was Thanksgiving. We thanked the rooster for his sacrifice and settled down to a dinner of juicy, tender meat, with sides of our home-grown broccoli and mashed potatoes.

The gravy, which happened almost by accident, was the most delicious I'd had in my life. It was just drippings and the white wine I'd put in the bottom of the pan to prevent burning, accented with the lemon, garlic, rosemary, and sage that I'd stuffed in the cavity. I thickened the juices with a sprinkling of flour, which gave the gravy the color and texture I remembered, and mellowed out the flavor a bit.

Emmett, vegan since he was sixteen, devoured the legs with gusto. Ever the finicky city girl, I stuck to the breast meat—which, though not as ample as the breast meat you'd get from a Cornish Cross, was entirely adequate.

The Buff Chanticleer fed us for a week. Roast chicken supper, chicken sandwiches, chicken noodle soup rich with marrow. Nothing went to waste, and we buried the remaining bones in the garden. And while we buried the bones out of respect for our rooster, I think that the truest sign of respect was having given this bird a contented life, at the end of which not a single part of him went to waste.

Chapter 10:

BOX OF BRASSICAS

· ·

Broccoli, Cauliflower, Kale, and Cabbage

Only miscreants survived the frost.

The mischievous chickens foraged in the crunchy grass, apparently unfazed by the chill of the ground beneath their bare, scaly claws. At night, they huddled together in the coop, sharing the heat generated by their clumped body mass. When I came in to check on them they moaned softly, a noise not of this world but somehow emanating from interrupted chicken dreams, whatever those may be—fierce foxes or endless yogurt fountains, hawks overhead or abundant juicy corn worms.

The bitter brassicas also shrugged off the season's new sparkle. The crystalline coating that adorned their leaves in the morning melted by midday, and they were none the worse for wear when their frosty garments dissolved. The brassicas stood in the middle of an apocalypse—the broccoli, cauliflower, kale, and cabbage green and bright despite the browned and withered tomato forest with its rotting fruits dripping from the brittle vines. The bean jungle had become skeletal. Dried pods rattled in the wind. And everywhere along the ground, the dead squash plants lay, waiting to trip passersby, their dark, hollow stems desiccated but wiry.

With the frost came wind and rainstorms blowing down from Canada or spiraling in from the Pacific. The rainwater beaded on the brassica leaves, and when the shiny balls were big enough, they rolled down to the center of the plant and dripped down to the roots, which in turn funneled the water back up to the pert, voluminous leaves.

And with the onset of storms, it felt like it was time for the farmers' markets to close up shop. But of course, the weather and the farmers' market don't always discuss timing with one another.

. . . .

I could definitely have been miserable. It was Saturday morning, and we were on our way to the Healdsburg farmers' market. Because it was so cold—a biting wind blew in the night before as clouds billowed in the northwest—we'd harvested all of the produce the day before and left it in the exterior refrigerator, a.k.a. the porch, covered with damp towels. At 8:00 a.m., the air hovered in the upper thirties, an entirely inappropriate temperature for coastal California. This wind must have been putting whitecaps on the Russian River—when gusts hit, our truck slipped sideways on the road. The fat-dropped rain had us flicking the windshield wipers as fast as they'd go.

But as we pulled into the parking lot, I had to smile. I get high on storms. I once spent five weeks at sea, and the highlight (certainly of the trip, and maybe of my life) was holding the helm and guiding a one-hundred-foot steel-hulled sailing ship through thirty-knot winds and twenty-foot swells. I'll never forget my determination as I focused all of my energy on maintaining the swinging compass's heading, while the boat was swept off course by a huge swell, corrected, overcorrected, and back again.

As we pulled into our usual spot, a pop-up tent across the way lifted up, skittered a few feet, and slammed into a van. My smile grew: the Healdsburg farmers' market looked like a sailboat caught in a squall. Canvas umbrellas swelled and took flight, vendors scurrying after to try and lash them down. Farmers huddled together, commiserating and trying to talk over wind that ripped their words and flung them to the sky. One wore a yellow rain suit—foulies, we called the rubber duck jackets and pants with their elastic cuffs and distinct lack of breathability that ensured that it rained both inside the suit and out.

I glanced over at Emmett, zipped up my rain jacket, and stepped outside. Within minutes my hair hung in wet ropes about my face, wind-whipped and sticking to my cheeks. What's the use of weather if you're not out in it anyway?

. . . .

Given the dangers of storm-tossed umbrellas and the consistency of the downpour, which hadn't let up for a single moment since we woke early this morning, we opted to miniaturize our farm stand. One table only so that everything could fit under our umbrella—our umbrella that wasn't waterproof or even water resistant, but would still, we hoped, shunt the majority of the rain to the side. No price signs because all of our signs were made of paper. It was technically illegal, but if we had put the signs out, the ink would have bled out either before or after the wind blew them away.

On display were the survivors of the season: brassicas, plus chard and storage crops. Winter is a challenging time for flora even in relatively mild northern California. Although we may not have blizzards or ice storms to contend with, we have chilly days and freezing nights: cause enough for plenty of plants to batten down the hatches and head below deck for the year. Frost wreaks havoc on those plants—like the squashes—that aren't equipped to deal with it. And the depressed temperatures, combined with fewer hours of daylight, slow down the metabolism and growth of any remaining frost-tolerant, edible plants. (Although somehow, it never seems to daunt the weeds.)

So it shouldn't come as a surprise that the most common method of surviving the winter is simply not to. While this route isn't the most convenient for herbivores or the carnivores that subsist on them, it actually works out just fine for plants. The individual plant dies, but its genetic material (ensconced in seeds or bulbs) chills, so to speak, until spring—when warmer temperatures trigger germination and the process begins again.

Some plants, however, have learned to live on the edge. By extending their growing season, they gain an advantage: the ability to function year-round. These frost-hardy warriors last longer, grow longer, and therefore have more energy available—energy that can transform into leaves for the farmer to harvest or from which to make seeds. They can function at a time when other plants die back, so there's less vertical competition for light. And they grow at a time when other plants have died and are in the process of releasing nutrients into the soil—a useful trick in nutrient-poor environments.

In order to reap these benefits, the plants have had to develop some form of frost, or even freezing, resistance. (Frost resistance and freezing resistance are different abilities; while

Ice crystals outlined each leaf of our baby lettuces during our first frost.

some plants can tolerate only light frosts, others can freeze solid and then spring back to life upon melting.) The processes that prevent freezing—the destruction of the plant on a violent cell-by-cell basis—are both molecular and miraculous.

Let's start with frost tolerance. Water famously freezes at 32 degrees F, but a water-based beer in the freezer won't solidify until it hits 28 degrees F or so. This is because alcohol has a significantly lower freezing point than water—about 200 degrees cooler, in fact. (Alcohol freezes at –173 degrees F.) So the alcohol content in the water acts as an antifreeze solution, allowing the water to supercool rather than crystallize.

Clearly, brassicas don't produce alcohol in their leaves; I think it's safe to say that if they did, the world would be a lot more excited to eat raw kale. But they do produce sugars and proteins that function similarly, and prevent the leaf from freezing if the temperature dips a bit below 32 degrees F.

If it gets cold enough, though, the antifreeze approach fails and the solution starts to solidify. If the plant is only frost tolerant, the proverbial beer bottle bursts. But some plants have developed an antifreezing or "cryoprotective" strategy. Basically, they take the cap off the beer bottle, let out enough beer so that the bottle doesn't break, and then suck the beer back in when the temperature is sufficiently warm for the solution to melt again.

Specifically, these plants extrude water from their cells as the temperature approaches freezing. The plants wilt as if they're crawling through a dessert, dried up and about to die. Tiny crevasses open up in the leaves to catch the escaping water. The plants freeze, but because there's hardly any water left in the cells, the cell walls don't break. Then, when the water melts, it's reabsorbed by the cells. The wilted plants spring back to life, pert, green, and ready to greet the day.

Which begs the question: Am I a brassica or a beer?

. . . .

Wormy corn's ability to drive customers away is nothing compared to what the rain can do, at least in fair-weather California. If you think you're the kind of person who would laugh about (and then devour) wormy corn, what would you do at 9 a.m. on a Saturday when the heavens have opened their floodgates and the farmers' market stands are threatening to lift off their moorings and float away down Healdsburg Avenue? Would you check your wallet for cash, don a rain slicker, grab your stoutest umbrella, and head to the car . . . or would the sound of the rain pounding the roof gently fade away as you cozy up in bed, wound tight in a comforter and lost in a book?

Perhaps in Oregon the customers possess more pluck, but in Healdsburg, few buyers set sail in the rain. As our first customer approached, suited up and clutching a drenched basket, I had to stifle the *Ahoy* that rose in my throat.

"Hi, Care!" Emmett shouted, recognizing the shrouded figure before I did.

"Hi guys," she replied. "Bit wet today, eh?"

Nearby, a farmer lifted the roof of her tent up with a stick, releasing a giant puddle of water that slammed into the asphalt.

"Thanks for coming," I said. "Not the best day for a market."

"Well, if you guys have to be here, we have to be here, too!" Care said.

And in one sentence, Care articulated the attitude that will make the local food movement stick. Although one wet weekend might not break a farm, a fair-weather attitude to local farming very well could. Does the recent popularity of local farms represent a permanent shift in production, or will the farm food fad fade? Farmers' markets have exploded in recent years, and so far the customer base has risen up to meet them. If that base disappears, thousands of new small farms will find themselves stranded: because farming is an investment meant to be recouped and borne out over time, it's not the sort of business that's easy to get into or out of. Economists might not care about the vagaries of their supply and demand curves, but I hope that we're not a country of economists. I have a hunch that the majority of Americans would feel a little tug at their heartstrings, were all the small farms in their neighborhoods to close up shop.

Care bought some broccoli and chard. As I watched customers in fogged-up cars rummage for umbrellas and steel themselves for their wet excursion, I was heartened by the fact that there were others like her. Over the course of the summer, I'd met people who felt that we needed backyard gardens and farm tours, local livestock and cheerful rows of wormy corn, so that future generations of children could experience a sense of America's history—and beyond that, an understanding that no matter how technologically advanced our society becomes, someone will still have to grow the food that feeds us all.

Customers laughed telling me stories about city kids who thought spaghetti grew on trees. And I laughed in turn when people wanted to buy my "rhubarb," which was actually rainbow chard. (I laughed partly because I'd be a fool to sell rhubarb with its deadly, poisonous leaves still attached to the stem.) But my younger self didn't know what chard was, let alone that its bright red stems bear some resemblance to rhubarb stalks. I may have gathered from the USDA food pyramid that spaghetti wasn't a fruit, and hence wasn't something that

Emmett thought that two broccoli heads were better than one.

grew on trees, but beyond that my knowledge of where food really came from ended at the grocery store receipt.

As a child, my only interaction with livestock came at the San Diego Zoo where, on a lucky day, you just might catch a chick hatching out of an incubator. They didn't mention that the chicks hatched were meat birds destined for the cheetah enclosure, but in retrospect I'm guessing that's the way it went. And rather than finding it repulsive, I think that's pretty damn cool. I'm no expert, but I think kids should know that it takes life to feed other life. For Thanksgiving this year, we bought a heritage turkey from a farmer just across the county border in Mendocino. He had two beautiful daughters, the smaller young enough to count her age out on one hand. She wore a floral print dress and smiled shyly as her dad explained that she was in charge of removing the gizzards from all of the turkeys they processed for customers that Thanksgiving. She wasn't traumatized; she was proud. And I'll bet she really enjoyed her Thanksgiving dinner.

There are plenty of farmers hoping that the country's new-found commitment to local production is a permanent shift. But customers have to be willing to participate in the local food system. Sometimes that involves a hatchet, but for starters, maybe just a rain jacket.

. . . .

Two hours later, the storm novelty wore thin. My pants were soaked through and my high-tech lightweight rain jacket had sprung a leak. I'd had the sense not to wear my traditional farmers' market Chacos, but not the sense to wear rubber boots. Thus, my lone pair of decent-looking closed toe shoes had morphed into a disaster of overstretched wet leather. My wool socks squished inside them, and I couldn't feel my toes, just a dull ache. (I might mention that when I was at sea, I was in the tropics. Warm and wet I can handle; cold and wet, not so much.)

But Care was not the only customer who showed up in the rain. Other regulars stopped by, smiles plastered to their wet faces, and as long as we kept talking, we were all proud of our collective bravery. The people who came made a point to buy something from every stand. The market manager told us not to worry about paying our stall fee, and thanked us for showing up in the rain. Some of the other farmers packed up early and headed home, but Emmett and I figured that since we were here, we might as well stay until the bitter end. And if my fingers and toes were wet and freezing, that was hardly anything compared to the sense of adventure. We were all in the same boat, farmers and customers—and we'd be here holding down our end of the line as long as they kept coming. We weren't at the bitter end just yet.

Chapter 11:

THE PRICE OF A RADISH (AND OTHER ROOTS)

·······································

Radishes, Beets, Carrots, and Potatoes

The last few minutes before market opening always pass like seconds. At 8:55 a.m., Emmett rushed around taping up price signs; I bunched bright stalks of rainbow chard, trying to strike a balance between efficiency and aesthetic.

"Four minutes until market," Emmett said, tapping his watch. "You know what they say—pile 'em high, and watch 'em fly."

In other words: worry about getting enough bunches on the table, and stop obsessing over each individual bunch. Market stands, including ours, strive for beauty in bounty because customers gravitate toward it. No one will pick a last lonely piece of produce—or even select from a few stragglers—but everyone relishes sorting through a big pile to find the best item.

I snapped rubber bands around the chard, placed the fifth bunch on the pile, and turned to the next green: Lacinato kale.

"How much are we charging for radishes today?" Emmett asked.

"Maybe we should come down to $1.50," I said, "But I hate doing that."

"Well, we can stick to $1.75, and if people complain, drop a quarter. We don't have that many bunches, anyway."

By 8:59 a.m., I'd bunched a few kales, thrown together four bags of baby lettuce mix, four of baby brassica mix, two of arugula, and I was working on the spinach. At 9:00 a.m., the start-of-market bell pealed: I was up to my elbows in green leaves, pulling spinach out of a harvest bin, tossing aside any stray weeds, and placing handfuls in bags.

Thirty seconds later, I put the last bag of spinach on display and fielded a salad purchase. It was one of our regulars: one half of an arugula-loving gay couple. He grabbed one bag of lettuce mix, one of arugula, and a bunch of beets. "How much are your radishes again? I remember last week they were on the expensive side," he said, in a friendly way.

I didn't mind him commenting on the price of our radishes: he was good-naturedly honest, and after all he was still buying other produce from our stand. He and I could agree to disagree on the cost, or I could take his advice to heart and drop the price a quarter or two—but he didn't make me feel embarrassed about my $1.75 radishes.

On the other hand, last week, when a well-clad woman toting a Starbucks cup picked up a bunch of radishes, asked the price, rolled her eyes, dropped the radishes onto the table, and walked off—*then* I felt embarrassed.

I'd been thinking about the incident ever since. Her coffee cup in particular gave me pause. This woman was happy to pay $4 for a cup of coffee (nutritional value: nil), but balked at the thought of shelling out $1.75 for a bunch of radishes (replete with Vitamin C and potassium, among other valuable nutrients).

Which explains why I'd been philosophizing about radishes all week—and yet still hadn't come up with a solid answer to Emmett's question. How much *should* we charge for radishes today? I supposed that it depended on the frame of reference. What you feel comfortable charging or what you are willing to pay comes down to which value—or valuation— system you subscribe to. And as a grower, my value system had definitely undergone a major shift from my days spent on the other side of the stand.

One way we could determine our radish price was using simple Econ 101: Supply and Demand. We could charge the price that rested at the intersection of the supply and demand curves: just what people were willing to pay for the amount of produce on offer, and no more. In the real world, which doesn't generally run according to economics graphs, this meant looking at our neighbors and charging what they were charging. (Or, if we wanted to get sneaky, a penny under.)

There was a bit of a problem with this simple system, though. Should we charge what our neighbors at the farmers' market were charging—or do we price our produce according to the supermarket sale at the Safeway across the street? Or at the health food store down the block? Was a radish just a radish, or were some radishes better than others? Was a farmers' market radish that was not organically certified (but was grown organically) of higher quality than an organically certified Safeway radish that was probably trucked in from Mexico?

Or we could look at our radish price from a grower's perspective. As a farmer, I have a distinct urge to charge people based on how difficult a given plant is to grow—and on whether or not it naturally replenishes itself. I'm happy to

Emmett washed and bunched French Breakfast radishes for market.

provide customers with big bunches of chard for $1.50, even though I've seen other stands charge $2 for half as much. Why? It's simple. Our chard plants will replace the leaves we harvested this morning by next week, and aren't likely to stop doing so anytime soon. Heck, if you drop by the field, I'll give it to you *free*.

On the other side of the spectrum sits the humble radish. Sure, it's a relatively quick grower: ready to go in a month or so. But like all roots and tubers, after I pluck it from the ground it's done. That bunch of French Breakfast radishes that I twist-tie together and place on the table won't give me seeds, won't resprout into a second radish crop, won't do anything other than remove nitrogen and potassium from my soil.

And *that* was the source of my radish angst. I looked at a bunch of radishes and thought: this is seven or eight entire plants. Seven or eight *lives*, if you want to get freaky about it. Was a quarter a plant too much to ask? (And really, what was the difference between $1.50 and $1.75 anyway, besides a sense of consumer pride?)

But that was applying an external moral framework, I know. It even dared to suggest that a commodity possesses intrinsic value, as opposed to simple market value.

There was one final valuation system we could consider— one that lay between the poetic farmer and the economist. It was based on fuzzy terms like quality, freshness, rarity, and even branding, but this system has weight in today's market. It suggests that a radish is a radish—but some radishes are better than others, and they come from better places.

First of all, there was the freshness angle. My radishes were plucked from the field that morning, placed under damp towels, and rushed to market; Safeway's were probably picked last week and refrigerated ever since. And my radishes were an heirloom French Breakfast variety—elongated, pink, with white at the top—whereas grocery stores usually stick to the run-of-the-mill round, maroon sort. Furthermore, customers were more than welcome to come visit my field, where they could question me about my growing practices. I doubt a grocery store would be so accommodating, because they probably have no idea who actually grows their produce. So my radish offered three things that other radishes didn't: guaranteed freshness, heirloom status, and complete openness about the story behind the food.

There were other, less tangible qualities about my produce, too. Shopping at the farmers' market is a feel-good experience. I'm not ashamed to admit it: there's absolutely a sense of charity, of supporting local farmers, in addition to the simple pleasure of attending a market—the music of the hometown band, the heaps of colorful vegetables, the artisanal cheeses, the aromatic bouquets of local flowers, the farmers who are willing to troubleshoot your backyard garden troubles or offer you tips for cooking summer squash. Many locals value this experience and the certainty that the produce they purchase is locally grown, knowing that the money they spend is going to a good cause. And for many customers, shopping at the farmers' market becomes a social outing and even something of a status symbol, a place to see and be seen by friends.

Even fuzzier, we already had customers who preferred our produce to that of other stands—or preferred us, or perhaps preferred our story of being young farmers just starting out. Part of that might have related to our "brand"—the real-life farm-startup adventures with which we regaled customers—but part of it did relate to tangible quality (and extra work on our part). We plucked our radishes at the peak of ripeness to ensure tender, crunchy roots, and we offered a variety of heritage radishes that customers couldn't get in the grocery store. Long, slender, blushing French Breakfast bunches were heaped next to the pert, festive little bouquets of white, lavender, and mauve Easter Egg bulbs. So perhaps a radish wasn't just a radish: there were radishes, and then there were fresh, local, heritage radishes, harvested when young and tender by young and tender (and slightly foolish) farmers.

It was about this time—mulling cost over in my head and trying to justify our prices—that I started to feel guilty again. Like I was part of some sort of liberal farming elite. Here I was, hoping to feed my local community—but in order to make money, I was charging folks a premium for local produce.

Who was, and wasn't, willing or able to pay that premium? Mirroring the different value systems were different types of customers. There were those who treated the farmers' market like a flea market, hunting around for the best prices. Then there were those who just walked around smiling, immersed in the experience, and bought whatever produce struck their fancy, from whatever farmer they happened to come across. And of course, there were the foodies, who usually had a farmer they'd frequented for years—and loved their piatta onions, or butter leaf lettuce, and bought it every week. But this sort also sometimes ventured around the market to find the best produce available, price be damned.

The final sort of customer was the bearer of the WIC (Women, Infants, and Children) certificate, who zeroed in on stands—like ours—that had posted WIC signs. They were limited to the stands that were enrolled in WIC—a government program that gives low-income mothers certificates with which to purchase fresh food at farmers' markets. Farmers weren't allowed to give them cash change for the certificates, so we'd throw in more produce until the total came to an even dollar amount.

Beets (taxonomically identical to chard) proved to be a good winter crop. They grew slowly but survived the frost.

So what was the optimal price for a radish? It depends on which customer you ask or which farmer. Should it be enough for me to live comfortably or enough for a working single mother to purchase it? Should there be a sliding scale? Some people consider the dollar, bandied about in a free market, to be their sole value system. But we don't provide emergency services only to those who can pay for them. People who can afford emergency rooms, firefighters, and policemen subsidize these services for those who can't. Society realizes that some commodities are life giving and therefore priceless. And what is food if not life?

Emmett was handling a transaction with a family friend, and another customer walked up. "How much for a bunch of radishes?" she asked me, peering at the price list to try to find it.

I sized her up: a sweatpants-wearing, toddler-toting mom. "For you," I say, "$1.25."

"I'll take a bunch," she said, "I love them with butter."

. . . .

Radishes survived long after fall's vibrancy had passed. Peppers and tomatoes had withered to the ground; corn leaves were wispy brown paper flecked with mildew, any abandoned ears shriveled and fuzzy inside. In the field, the radishes remained, accompanied by other survivors like kale, chard, beets, and broccoli. Frost tolerant, these lucky few would last the California winter into the next spring.

The local farmers' markets had closed with the proverbial whimper. In the last weeks, they had been more craft showcases than a place to purchase local produce. Even the farmers turned artisan, peddling garlic braids and handmade wreaths, wool blankets from their sheep, shellacked gourds cut into birdhouses. Most customers were more excited to start Christmas shopping than to start eating lots of kale, and who could blame them? To tell you the truth, we were excited to set our sights on Christmas and bid the farmers' market farewell. 'Tis the season, and all that. We were tired and needed the rest. We were ready to have a few months where we could be normal people, sleeping in on the weekends, rising after the sun does, going outside on our own terms instead of the market's.

With the farmers' markets closed, we were selling produce to customers whose e-mail addresses we'd gathered in the last few weeks before the market's demise. We'd e-mail out the week's availability to these customers, and they'd e-mail in their order. We harvested for them and left the produce in the basement with an honor system jar for collecting money.

It was a Sunday, and Emmett asked me to help him harvest an order for the Green Grocer (a local grocery store that carries only foods produced within 250 miles of the store's geographic location). They'd requested our radishes and arugula, so on a frosty, foggy winter morning, we drove down to the field. I was bundled up in jeans, a pajama shirt I'd worn to bed, and two jackets, a scarf wrapped around my neck and a wool hat pulled down over my unwashed hair. Emmett asked if I'd mind harvesting the radishes.

When it's cold and wet, I much prefer yanking out roots to snipping salad greens, so I began busily pulling up French Breakfast radishes, selectively harvesting only the largest specimens. As I moved down the row, Emmett called out and suggested that I start at the base of the row and harvest every single plant. "We have a lot of radishes ready right now," he said, "so let's just pull them all."

Emmett's always trying to tell me how to harvest. Really, who crowned him the farmer king? Why can't he just let me do things *my* way?

I good-naturedly grumbled, but left it at that. Opting out of the argument rather than into it (a rare move on my part), I relented and restarted the harvest at the beginning of the row. As I pulled out the radishes with my right hand, I transferred them into a large bunch in my left, holding them by the greens for easy washing later. A flash caught my eye, and I noticed something strange around one of the bulbs.

"Um," I said aloud, "There's a ring on this one."

As I was trying to figure out how a ring had ended up on a radish—and starting to realize that perhaps it wasn't accidental—Emmett materialized by my side and asked me to marry him. I was unshowered, wearing clothes I'd slept in, with hands dirty from harvesting radishes. I said yes, or something like it. He picked me up in a great bear hug and spun me around the field. Everything so barren and empty, just the four rows of overwintering crops—but already tiny green stitches in the space that was ploughed under, wild mustard greens and bell beans sprouting that would be hip-high by spring.

He put me back down. In the gray world, we kissed for a while.

"Really?" I asked. "What made you decide now was the right time?"

That day, Emmett explained, was the four-year anniversary of our first date. There was no Green Grocer order; Emmett had made it up. And he'd placed the ring on a radish seedling three weeks earlier so the plant would grow up around the ring, holding it in place when I pulled it.

And the timing—well, it just felt right. He was ready. I always had been.

The next few hours before we started making the requisite phone calls were ours. We decided to celebrate by taking the rest of the day off. This was new territory, but we spent the afternoon at a familiar place: the fish hatchery at Lake Sonoma. We'd been there many times before, and had a knack for visiting when the museum and hatchery were closed and there was absolutely nothing to see. But it was winter, the river was high, and the salmon were starting to move. We stood on a bridge, lording over the dark pools of the fish ladder, squinting to try and catch sight of a salmon swirling in the current. After a while, we walked through the hatchery proper, out back to the blue grow-out tanks full of young salmon that would be released later in the season.

A river otter slipped into one of the tanks, nabbed his pescetarian lunch, and, fish in mouth, shimmied out of the tank. He waltzed across the sidewalk and scampered back behind a "Wilderness Rehabilitation—Keep Out" sign. On the cement he left behind perfect wet paw-prints and a telltale dotted line of drops from the fish's tail.

A lucky otter, I thought, to have his meal contained in those convenient tanks. And then I realized that we weren't so different. Like the otter, we could dash across the road any time we wanted and find ourselves surrounded by bounty— before disappearing back into our native habitat, our cozy little place that was starting to feel like home. Of course, his miracle was in the move from hunter-gatherer to inadvertent farmer. His food supply was secure, as long as his humans continued to tend it. My miracle was in my move backward—from a macaroni-and-cheese punk rocker who uprooted strawberries, to a woman who could coax green things out of the ground and onto dozens of families' plates. A woman who just might end up a farmer's wife, after all.

I looked from where the otter had vanished to the humble silver ring on my hand. It didn't fit on my ring finger (which Emmett had guessed to be the size of his pinky), so it was on my middle finger instead. The Starbucks woman, the WIC mothers, the foodies: concepts of cost melted away. That particular radish? This simple ring? Some things are beyond concepts of price.

Chapter 12:

DAIRY DEVILS

· ·

Rotating Ruminants

No sooner had we gotten engaged than I set out to convince Emmett that we should have kids. Seven of them. My argument went something like this.

Vegetables: check. Fruits: check. Roots, tubers, bulbs: check, check, check. Eggs: check. And yet didn't it seem like our farm was missing something? Our house was surrounded by grassy hillsides that had been grazed down by the rabid cows that had nearly crushed me in an attempt to wrest corn stalks from the truck. At first, I thought that maybe it was sheep we were lacking. Or perhaps a sheepdog.

Sheep, I reasoned, would be relatively low maintenance. They'd keep the grasses neatly trimmed. The breed I selected—Babydoll Southdowns, a heritage English breed that is petite enough to weed beneath grapevines—was in hot demand in the Sonoma wine country, and the lambs sold for as much as $750 per animal. I could sell any lambs that were born and make a little money off my livestock, which would also function as something for a dog to herd.

Actually, to be perfectly honest, I can't remember which argument I took. I wanted a herding dog, so we needed sheep for her—or I wanted sheep, so I needed a herding dog. I may have taken different tactics at different times. Regardless, the growing menagerie somehow provided justification for purchasing itself and the sheep and Aussie puppy arrived on our farm around the same time.

The failed sheep experiment began with a breeding trio of Babydoll Southdown sheep inelegantly stuffed in the back of our pickup truck, to the great delight of our wiggly puppy, Kea, perched between us on the armrest. Three sheep: one male, Teddy, who would turn out to be further proof of my male livestock hypothesis; and two pleasantly timid ewes. I say "pleasantly timid" because the only thing worse than a stupid, fearful sheep is a stupid, aggressive sheep. Or, as Monty Python put it, "That most dangerous of animals . . . the clever sheep."

At first I was awed by the sight of the sheep grazing the hillside behind our house. How perfectly pastoral, I thought. Boy, were we real farmers, or what? Even Emmett agreed that the sight of the sheep wandering through tall grasses at sunset was a little slice of heaven. The bleating was pleasant (from far away, anyway), a soothing sound straight out of Wordsworth's hills.

It took me several weeks before I started to realize what many a farmer already knows: sheep suck.

Unlike chickens, sheep have the personality of a spoon. I know that a handful of shepherds may argue with me, but I'm pretty sure that the majority of them would agree wholeheartedly—and that, like me, they end up tolerating sheep because they love their herding dog. Or maybe they delight in mutton or lamb. Or they inherited a sheep farm and haven't been able to find an idiot to buy it. Or perhaps, for some unfathomable reason, they prefer the aggravating bleat of a hungry sheep to the annoying drone of a lawnmower.

Neither Emmett nor I had ever kicked or hit an animal before; it just wasn't in our character. But on separate occasions, we each took a whack at Teddy. It is extremely difficult to avoid hurting an animal that has just pummeled you with all the force in his hefty, stocky body—has in fact knocked you to the ground that he has conveniently just shat upon—and is backing up to do it again with a look in his eye that comes straight from hell. We figured we needed to go Cesar Milan on his ass: teach him that we, and not he, were the top rams in the flock.

Unfortunately, performing self-defense karate on Teddy was like kicking a boulder. It hurt the foot far more than the ram. Actually, kicking Teddy was worse than kicking a rock: rocks don't laugh at you. After what I thought was a powerful counter-attack—his head meeting my sole instead of its intended destination, which was the soft spot behind my knees—Teddy would wiggle his tail, which seemed to be ovine for, "Hee hee; that tickles, silly human." Then he'd use me as a scratching post and rub his oily, snotty nose on my leg. Then, if I turned my back, the rat bastard ottoman of a sheep would ram me again.

We soon gave up on teaching Teddy a lesson and learned to live in fear of the sound of rapid hoof-beats. Jokes about mutton assuaged my damaged farm ego, although we had no serious intention of eating Teddy. Instead, we kept him long enough to impregnate the ewes, and then got rid of him on Craigslist.

Apparently it wasn't sheep we were missing. We needed something better: kids. Really, what could be cuter than a kid snuggling with a puppy? We could lock them in the dog crate together so they'd bond with one another. Perfect.

....

And so Ginger entered our lives. When she came home to us she was only about four pounds, bound to her bottle but clearly ready to take on the world. We tucked her into a little bed on the floor, but she immediately got up. She leapt onto the couch and from there to the coffee table, where she scared the living daylights out of our lazy house cat. Jasper fled with fluffed fur and a sulking look that I took to mean, "First a puppy, and now what the hell is this thing?"

Our beleaguered puss had never before come into contact with a Nigerian Dwarf goat kid. Before I went to pick Ginger up from a nearby family farm, neither had I. But as usual, I had performed plenty of research to determine that the Nigerian Dwarf goat was just the right fit for our farm. Originally imported from West Africa in the 1930s, Ginger's ancestors were destined to be conveniently sized zoo food. Over time, artificial selection of the heritage stock resulted in two different breeds that eventually came to be recognized by the national goat registries: Pygmy (a mini meat goat, short and comically stocky) and Nigerian Dwarf (a mini dairy goat, more Barbie than Ken: fine-boned, slender, and possessed of extremely capacious udders).

Nigerian Dwarfs—or Nigis, as the obsessed affectionately call them—have enjoyed soaring popularity in recent years. Their small stature and gregarious personalities have made them homestead favorites: like chickens, they excel as both pet and producer. And like heritage breed poultry, they are

Ginger loved using Teddy as a playground—one of the better uses for male livestock I've seen.

sufficiently varied so that owners quickly succumb to a "collect them all" mentality.

Unlike certain goat breeds—for instance, the all-white Saanen—there is no color standard for Nigerian Dwarf goats. Each one is different. They come in black, gold, red, white, dark buckskin, chocolate buckskin, cou clair (pale front quarters shading to black hindquarters), Swiss (black and tan, patterned after the Alpine goat), silver, brown, and chamoisee (tan with dark feet, belly, back stripe, and face). And each of these colors can be moon spotted (dabbed with colored spots), broken with white (patches of white in the midst of a pattern), broken with excessive white (large patches of white dominating a pattern), and accompanied by brown, gold, or blue eyes. Each goat's appearance is as unique as his or her personality, and personalities run the gamut from reserved but tolerant of human contact to lapdog attention whore. The majority of Nigerians fall on the latter end of the spectrum.

There are other reasons Nigis make excellent backyard livestock. While full-sized dairy goats can weigh a couple of hundred pounds, a Nigerian gal might top out at fifty pounds and take up approximately the same amount of space as a Labrador retriever. They eat a third of the feed of a regular sized dairy goat, so they're cheaper to maintain. And thanks to their diminutive stature, they're easy to handle, even for kids—making them a popular choice in 4H and FFA families. Best of all, the market isn't yet saturated for these goats, which means it's fairly easy to place all offspring into loving homes: female kids can be sold off as family milkers, while male kids can be castrated and sold off as weedwhacking pets. In other words, unlike many 4H and FFA projects, your baby doesn't turn into sausage.

There's another reason that goats are attractive, at least from a writer's perspective. The goat world possesses its own charismatic language. There is, of course, the goat kid: the only young animal to have bequeathed its name to human children. Goat kids can be further broken down into doelings, bucklings, and goatlings. (Try adding that suffix to any monosyllabic word, and you'll find it instantly becomes 50 percent cuter.) Elegantly, their parents are the female doe and the male buck. Beats the hell out of cow and bull, one of which is frequently used pejoratively and the other of which is typically followed by "shit." Ewe, ram, and lamb are similarly dull.

And I haven't even touched on the verbs. A goat giving birth and commencing lactation is said to "freshen." (Try that one out on a pregnant woman: "Baby, don't think of it as labor; you're just freshening.") Therefore, first-time mothers are "first fresheners"; after freshening, they're also called "senior does."

Prepositions assume new importance. A kid's pedigree is described as "out of" the dam, "by the" sire. As in, Ginger is out of Gravenstein Apple by Guy Noir, who is out of Raven. So in one sentence, you have ascertained the two most important parts of her pedigree: her parents, and her paternal grandparents. The paternal granddam is particularly important because the most important part of a dairy goat is her udder—and since bucks don't have udders, the potential worth of a sire is tied to his mother's name and reputation, until such time as he has produced enough show-winning daughters to stand on his own.

And of course, while cows are bovines and sheep are ovines, goats are caprines. The word capers right into "capricious," an adjective that helps explain why both human and goat children came to be referred to as kids. Goat kids and human kids share that unique attention span that is at times nonexistent and at others entirely persistent. Ginger, once she discovers the presence of chicken feed in the chicken coop, will devote her life to trying to get at it. Like the child who has to be read *Goodnight Moon* every free moment for months on end, Ginger seizes every opportunity she has to escape from the pasture and beeline it for the coop. But try getting a goat or a child to do what you want and, if it's not what they want, you'll find the sensation akin to repeatedly thwacking your head against a wall. In short order, Emmett and I trained our dog Kea to jump up only on command ("Dance!"). But when we attempted to convince a doeling not to jump up on us, it was like playing whack-a-mole. We pushed the goat off. We gently rapped her on the nose. And like clockwork, her adorable little cloven hooves popped right back up, stamping our thighs in mud and mashed-up goat pellets. (Ah, goat pellets.

Another reason that goats beat the heck out of cows. Like sheep, they defecate in convenient, inoffensive, dry pellets.)

A Saanen, the Holstein of the goat world, can produce seventeen pounds of milk per day, while a highly productive Nigerian might produce five. And although you might think that more milk is better, that's not necessarily true for the home goat keeper unless he or she happens to have swine to feed all the extra milk to. And there's a difference in milk quality, too, which is important for the home cheese maker. The Nigerian's milk has the highest butterfat content of any of the dairy goats, so there is less whey byproduct.

Which reminds me, I haven't yet gotten around to making that chèvre—but that's something I could get into.

. . . .

Ginger was quickly followed by Sedona, Pippi, Calamari, Zoe, Tuxedo, E squared (Emily and Elizabeth, purchased as prenamed adults), and our aspiring herd sire, Gobi. Aspiring because when he came home, Gobi weighed just a few pounds, his testicles were the size of peanuts, and based on an embarrassing accident perpetrated on my lap on the three-hour drive home—he managed to diarrhea all over me as soon as we pulled away from his farm—it was amply clear that he wasn't going to be seeing much action anytime soon.

"You brought home another one that needs a bottle?" Emmett asked, shaking his head. "I thought they were all going to be weaned."

Surprise!

"And wait a second. How many goats do you have in the car? You said you were only getting three."

Surprise!

"Four. But this one reminded me of Tux."

Word to the wise: never buy animals while in a state of grief. To do so is to ensure that common sense will be subsumed by the desire to fill aching voids with adorable creatures. A couple of weeks before bringing home our new goats, we left for the weekend to attend Emmett's cousin's wedding ceremony. It was an agonizing decision: although I wanted to accompany Emmett to the wedding, leaving the animals—and the vegetables—in the care of someone else is stressful. We provided our caretakers with written and verbal instructions, physical demonstrations, and reminded them multiple times to check under the porch for eggs and broody chickens who'd been trying to spend the night down there. And then, after shelling out fifty dollars per night for the service, we worried about the farm the entire time we were gone.

When we arrived back home at midnight—after a five-hour flight and an hour-long drive from the airport—we went straight to the coop to check on the girls. Hope? Check. Joy? Check. Two Wyandottes? Check. Tux? I ran my hand over every single chicken in the coop, climbing into the back corners to see if for some reason she was there instead of on her usual perch in the front. But Tux was missing. We spent two and a half hours with flashlights searching for her in the dark and calling her name. I was crying even before Emmett found her wings, head, and feet—the spine there, too, but the torso skinned and disemboweled—across the road in the vineyard. We buried her that night.

The caretakers hadn't collected a huge pile of eggs that were beneath the porch—which would have further persuaded broody Tux to try sitting on them overnight instead of returning to the coop, where she would have been protected from predators—and clearly failed to follow verbal and written instructions.

Emmett felt terrible. This had been my worst fear before leaving for the wedding. So he couldn't exactly begrudge me a black goat with a little white star on her head who followed me around like a puppy dog and climbed into my lap.

. . . .

Life with seven kids quickly settled into sweet, comforting farm routine. I quickly learned their language—the "mehh" that meant, "Hi, mom!" or the "MEH!" that meant, "More alfalfa, please, we're out!" I could tell them apart by the sounds of their voices—Tuxedo's shrill urgency, which hovered somewhere between a yodel and a bleat, Pippi's piercing whine, Sedona's reserved, polite call.

They progressed quickly into puberty, and before I knew it, the girls were humping each other while, in a separate pasture, Gobi watched them and licked his penis. When we placed Elizabeth in the pasture with him, she was approximately twice his size, and Gobi seemed to prefer watching the doelings hump each other to mating with Mrs. Robinson. We were eager for him to impregnate a female goat, because we wanted to start milking as soon as possible.

And then one day, a fascinating awakening took place before our eyes, or at least before Emmett's eyes. I was at work—I had taken an office job to fund our off-season investments in seeds and livestock—when I received an e-mail entitled "In other bright news." Emmett typically writes in grammatically correct sentences, and he's not normally prone to graphic description of any sort, so this e-mail was rather out of character.

Sedona, Tuxedo, and Gobi. This photo sums up Tuxedo's personality perfectly.

"Gobi just jizzed all over the place. He had a look of pure ecstasy on his face but he missed his target."

To which I responded, "Where was the target at the moment of lift-off?"

"She was forward and to the right," Emmett wrote. "He tried to mount her twice, but bounced off both times. The first time got his winky excited. And the second time when he landed it just went shooting all over, and he arched his head up with his lips curled back and quivering and his teeth exposed, saying to himself, thank you God. By the way, she seems interested now, they were doing funny vibrating tongue things at each other."

Upon my return, I watched Gobi try to mate with Elizabeth. He thrust forward and then fell backward, twisting in an attempt to land on his feet. I thought about placing a box behind Elizabeth, for him to step up on, but I was afraid it might ruin the moment. Also, it would have been creepy.

You might think it's sick, but trust me, if you had goats, you'd watch them having sex, too. First of all, it's important to know when breeding has taken place: goat kids should arrive 145 days after copulation, and the human midwife must be ready to help out. And second of all, it's like your very own, real-life Discovery Channel. We don't have television, and it's these little hilarities that I miss every moment I'm away from the farm.

· ·

There's one thing about the farm that's a little bit terrifying. Somehow the days start to race down a runway and soar up over me—and suddenly little Tuxedo, the coltish black fuzz-ball, has twin doelings of her own and the udder to match. So does her best friend, Sedona, who is and always will be the prima donna of the herd. Long, elegant, and refined—"very dairy," as goat people would say—she's a movie star and she knows it. But she's no longer standing on the roof of the goat house arching her long neck and basking in the admiration of her herd and her humans: she's too busy admiring her own two doe kids, one of whom is a perfect miniature of herself, the other an exact (but feminine) replica of the father. Ginger, who once shared a bottle with Gobi—and has missed him since he was separated off from the females; they often flirt through the fence—is now pregnant by him, expecting mini-Gobis of her own.

And so I thank the stars for the seasons, because without waypoints, this would all pass too quickly. I'm glad for the bud-break of the grapevines in March, the first Pruden's Purple tomato in August, the brilliant frosts of October, and the reddening leaves of November. And I'm thankful for the weather and the difficulties and the fact that I am out in both of them, daily confronting the living and dying that allows us all to survive. Watching the sky clear after a storm, the sun setting behind the hills of gray-green oaks, I will always miss the ocean a little bit—that sense of possibility and unknown that I've traded for a hundred daily certainties and a warm bed.

But that vast emptiness is just a short drive away, as it is no matter where we live. And while we may take only occasional trips to the sea, the squalls that wash ashore remind us that we never have the remotest idea what's going to happen. For all the chores and simple pleasures of farm life, the details that consume our daily existence, the sea is always there, in the same way that those we lose will always remain with us.

I am still inconsolable over some of the animals that have passed away under my care. Even if their deaths weren't my fault, their lives will always be my responsibility. The trouble with animal husbandry is this: killing creatures is easy when you view them as objects. It's harder, but in many ways better, when you know them and take good care of them. And when a farm animal you've loved unexpectedly dies, even if that creature is a seemingly simple chicken, a piece of you goes with her. While the shock grows more distant, the legend only swells with time: those small chicken lives, forever a part of the soil and the flora-fauna-human family that make up a farm. A hundred animals and a handful of ghosts.

So what does a farmer, faced with the loss of a pet chicken, do? Buy a goat and name her after the chicken. (And rejoice when the goat has the same utterly unquenchable lapdog spirit that the chicken did.) What does a farming couple, not earning quite enough money at the farmers' market to make a living, do? Start a CSA, branch out into dairy, host wwoofers, build a barn, raise heritage turkeys.

There's no question that we'll make this work. I've finally found a vocation where it's completely reasonable—expected, even—to be a stubborn idiot. And I've found a wonderfully stubborn idiot to enjoy this vocation with, one who rises at 6:30 a.m. in the off-season to build a barn for the goats, and who can be found in the middle of a rainstorm lashing tarps to that as-yet-unroofed barn and frantically swabbing the decks—er, mopping the plywood floor.

From the table in the living room where I write, I look out the kitchen window. At the very top of the frame, goat feet scamper back and forth across the base of a hill. I hear a hen announce—bokbokBAGAWK—that she's laid an egg, and a young Silver Sebright cockerel attempt to crow. (He sounds like a gagging power drill.) And you know what? Call me crazy, call me poor, call me covered in chicken shit. Call me tired, call me scared, call me satisfied, call me passionate. And did I mention crazy?

Go ahead. But before you do, let me offer you a few eggs and a pair of Chihuahua-sized goat kids, and then we'll see who's crazy. Trust me, you don't have to like worms, or even fresh tomatoes. There's a little farm in all of us.

FRUITS OF LABOR

As of this writing, Foggy River Farm is three years old. Still selling at the Healdsburg farmers' market and now offering a CSA program, too. Farm to Pantry gleaners visit regularly; several friends contribute labor in exchange for produce; vineyard workers have set up a small community garden adjacent to the field. We've hosted a number of wwoofers and longer-term interns who have left far more than just footprints on the farm.

In April 2010, we held our wedding ceremony and reception down at the field. The wedding party rode in on a neighbor's horse-drawn wagon: a service that had been provided in exchange for an old tractor. The tables were decorated with farm tools, eggs, and produce. We married shortly after becoming goat grandparents: movie star Sedona and her two-week-old twin doelings joined us at the field and punctuated the ceremony with the occasional "meh." One of them, Misa—a lapdog doeling we named after another lost friend, an adopted feral cat named Mouse who passed away—features prominently in our wedding photos. Her sister went to another family to become a backyard pet milker, but Misa will stay with us, and we hope she'll soon give us our first great grandkids. She and Tie, Tuxedo's kid who also stayed with us, are the best of friends, just like their mothers.

In other firsts, I made my inaugural chèvre, and it was fantastic: raw and savory and decidedly chèvre tasting, not terribly different in flavor from the artisanal store-bought varieties. But it meant so much more and therefore tasted so much better. It carried with it the frustration of a kicked bucket and the patience required to train the first fresheners, the memory of the soothing, quiet mornings in the milkroom and the gentle psh-psh into the stainless steel pail, the satisfaction of a full udder deflating and a bucket filling.

Did I mention the sheep are growing on me? My first chèvre was even made of half Babydoll Southdown milk—which, I suppose, makes it technically not a true chèvre. Though we eventually gave up on milking the sheep, it's nice, actually, to have a few animals that are reasonably predictable and low-maintenance. The goats and chickens pride themselves on their ability to create chaos, but the sheep focus on simply existing. And these days, the sheep exist even more comfortably with the companionship of our two gay alpacas, Ben and Humble. (And yes, I'm quite sure they're gay. My gay ex-boyfriend suggested that they might just be bros, but I pointed out that bros don't typically hump each other, neck, and watch each other pee.) Teddy mellowed out and joined another farm; in fact, we traded him for the alpacas, thanks to Craigslist.

And so it is that, after much hemming and hawing, we're putting down roots. We have a permanent space now: a patch of earth surrounded by a stout fence and watered with irrigation pipes that will never have to be moved. Emmett's parents have carved out a corner of the vineyard for us, and we're starting to put in some permanent crops of our own: berries, fruit trees, artichokes, asparagus. We've even built two barns—one animal, one vegetable. (The vegetable barn was finished just in time for our wedding reception barn dance.)

I don't get away much. It's not just that it's hard to leave the farm—which it is, since we're responsible for so many lives—but it's hard to afford to leave the farm, too. Between the Healdsburg farmers' market, our CSA program, and the animals, we gross about $30,000 a year. That's before we pay for seeds, irrigation supplies, chicken feed, hay, and the barns required to house the animals and equipment. We're working on increasing our CSA membership and boosting farmers' market sales so that we can subsist entirely on farm income, but in the meantime, I work as a reporter for the local paper and write whenever and wherever I can. Not that writers make much more than farmers, but every little bit helps.

Being anchored to one spot is a little bit lonely and a little bit lovely. While I do occasionally wish I could shove off and sail around the world, there's something to be said for loving where you live. The oak and eucalyptus trees, the morning fog, the wide-open spaces: all have become familiar. A host of four-legged and feathered friends greets me every time I open my front door. I know every curve of Eastside Road; the sudden rumble as my station wagon banks left onto our dirt driveway signifies that I'm home. When I rattle to a stop, I look for Emmett's pickup truck—either parked in the driveway or a barely visible speck across the road and down the hill. We got the truck for a good price because it had been in a fender bender, which means some panels were replaced and even after two years, they still haven't been painted. The hood is starting to rust and it's like a hundred other things that fall to the wayside, below the farming priority list. Our house is rarely tidy because a clean milk room and chicken coop are more important. Our Christmas lights stay up year-round and our first mistletoe is still taped to a doorjamb, but every evening we gather the day's eggs and shut the coop door. Four months after our wedding, we were still working on our thank-you notes, although we managed to raise an entire barn in just over two.

But—and this is a big confession for a San Diego girl—I don't mind being a little bit redneck. Like the goats and the chickens, the tomatoes and the lettuces, I'm a happy creature of routine. Every day, Tuxedo starts her soprano trilling at 6:00 a.m.: a morning milk-me serenade. I don't even hear the roosters anymore; they're impotent in comparison. If we don't hear her, Emmett and I start worrying about coyotes, and one of us will slip out of the warm bed and walk over to the front door to peer into the chilly morning. Each time we do, she bursts into song.

Home feels like the whole world, and the whole world feels like home.

ENDNOTES
·························

1. United States Census, "Data Set: 2006-2008 American Community Survey 3-Year Estimates." 997,082 Individuals employed in "Farming, fishing, and forestry occupations." 143,195,793 total civilian employed population.

2. United States Department of Agriculture, Economic Research Service, Data Set: Foreign Agricultural Trade of the United States (FATUS), www.ers.usda.gov/data/FATUS.

3. National Ag Safety Database, "Older Farmers: Factors Affecting Their Health and Safety," http://nasdonline.org.

4. United States Department of Agriculture, Agricultural Marketing Service, "USDA Announces that National Farmers' market Directory Totals 6,132 Farmers' markets," www.ams.usda.gov.

5. United States Department of Agriculture, Economic Research Service, "State Fact Sheets: California," www.ers.usda.gov/statefacts /ca.htm. Average age of principal farm operator in 2007: 58.4.

6. Texas A&M Agricultural Extension, "Universal Boon to the Salad Bowl," http://plantanswers.tamu.edu/publications/vegetabletravelers /lettuce.html.

7. Thomas Jefferson Foundation, "'Tennis Ball' Lettuce (*Lactuca sativa*)," http://explorer.monticello.org.

8. Agricultural Marketing Resource Center, "Lettuce Profile," www.agmrc .org.

9. Michael Pollan, *The Omnivore's Dilemma: A Natural History of Four Meals* (New York: Penguin, 2006), 165.

10. University of California Vegetable Research and Information Center, "Leaf Lettuce Production in California," http://vric.ucdavis.edu. According to the Center, lettuce should be "vacuum cooled" after harvesting and then stored just above freezing at 98 percent relative humidity. It "may be held for 2 to 3 weeks at 34 degrees F," but "at 27 degrees F, shelf life is reduced to 1 to 2 weeks."

11. United States Census of Agriculture, "Table 34. Vegetables, Potatoes, and Melons Harvested for Sale: 2007 and 2002" (2007), www.agcensus .usda.gov.

12. United States Department of Agriculture, National Agricultural Statistic Service, www.nass.usda.gov. In 2008, California loose leaf lettuce industry had a $305-million value.

13. United States Environmental Protection Agency, Office of Pesticide Programs, "Carbaryl IRED Facts," www.epa.gov.

14. Associated Press, "Worst Industrial Disaster Still Haunts India" (December 2, 2009), www.msnbc.msn.com.

    Ingrid Eckerman, *The Bhopal Saga—Causes and Consequences of the World's Largest Industrial Disaster* (India: Universities Press, 2005).

15. Thompson, et al, "Pesticide Take-Home Pathway Among Children of Agricultural Workers: Study Design, Methods, and Baseline Findings," *Journal of Occupational and Environmental Medicine* 45:1 (2003), 42–53.

16. Lu, et al, "Pesticide Exposure of Children in an Agricultural Community: Evidence of Household Proximity to Farmland and Take Home Exposure Pathways," *Environmental Research* Section A 84 (2000), 290–302.

17. Curl, et al, "Evaluation of Take-Home Organophosphorus Pesticide Exposure among Agricultural Workers and Their Children," *Environmental Health Perspectives* 110(12) (December 2002), 787–792.

18. Columbia University, Center for Environmental Research and Conservation, "Introduced Species Summary Project: Giant Marine Toad (*Bufo marinus*)," www.columbia.edu.

19. United States Census of Agriculture, "Summary by Age and Primary Occupation of Principal Operator: 2007" (2007), www.agcensus.usda .gov. Thirty-two percent of America's youngest farmers—thirty-four years old or younger—are tenant farmers.

20. For examples of specific young farmers raising chickens, please see Provenance Farm in Oregon (http://rachelprickett.wordpress.com /about), Mighty Food Farm in Vermont (http://mightyfoodfarm .com), and Blue Fox Farm in Missouri (www.bluefoxfarm.net).

21. Louis P. Tremante, "Livestock in nineteenth century New York City," *Urban Agriculture Magazine*, www.ruaf.org.

22. Jessica Bennett, "The New Coop De Ville: The Craze for Urban Poultry Farming," *Newsweek* (November 17, 2008), www.newsweek.com.

23. American Farm Bureau, "Young Farmers and Ranchers Anticipate Bright Future," *The Voice of Agriculture* (March 18, 2008), www.fb.org.

24. United States Department of Agriculture Economics, Statistics, and Market Information System, National Agricultural Statistics Service, "Farm Computer Usage and Ownership," http://usda.mannlib .cornell.edu.

25. See note 22.

26. United States Department of Agriculture, National Agricultural Statistics Service. "Statistics by Subject: National Statistics for Chickens." www.nass.usda.gov.

27. United States Department of Agriculture Economics, Statistics, and Market Information System, National Agricultural Statistics Service, "Chickens and Eggs Annual Summary" (February 2010), http://usda .mannlib.cornell.edu.

28. Bernard E. Rollin, *Animal Rights & Human Morality* (Amherst, New York: Prometheus Books, 2006).

29. G. M. Jones, "Guidelines to Culling Cows with Mastitis" (Virginia Tech, May 1999), http://pubs.ext.vt.edu/404/404-204/404-204.html.

30. Berton Roueche, Annals of Medicine, "Something a Little Unusual," *The New Yorker* (May 15, 1965), 180, www.newyorker.com.

31. United States Department of Agriculture, Economic Research Service, "Food Spending in American Households, 2003–04," www.ers.usda .gov. Average annual spending per person on tomatoes: $14.44.

32. Frameworks Institute, "How Did This Broccoli Get on My Plate? Framing Food as a Public Issue," www.frameworksinstitute.org /workshops/broccoli.

33. U.S. Census Bureau, 2010 Statistical Abstract, Arts, Recreation, and Travel: Recreation and Leisure Activities, "Table 1213. Sporting Goods Sales by Product Category: 1990 to 2007, and Projection, 2008," www.census.gov.

34. HighBeam Business, "Industry Report: Chewing Gum," http://business .highbeam.com. According to the report, total retail sales of gum in the U.S. in 2001 reached $2.8 billion.

35. James E. Deitz and James L. Southam, *Contemporary Business Mathematics for Colleges* (Mason, Ohio: Cengage Learning, 2008).

36. Society of St. Andrew, www.endhunger.org.

37. Meg McConahey, "Sharing the Bounty," *Santa Rosa Press-Democrat* (November 26, 2008), www.pressdemocrat.com.

38. See note 36.

39. Personal correspondence with WWOOF USA representative (November 2008).

40. Ric Bessin, "Sweet Corn Pests," University of Kentucky College of Agriculture, www.ca.uky.edu/entomology.

41. Peter A. Peterson and Angelo Bianchi, *Maize Genetics and Breeding in the 20th Century* (Singapore: World Scientific Publishing Company, 1999).

42. United States Department of Agriculture, National Agricultural Statistics Service, Quick Stats, www.nass.usda.gov/quickstats.

43. United States Department of Agriculture, National Agricultural Statistics Service, Quick Stats, www.nass.usda.gov/quickstats. Includes both fresh and processing corn.

44. David Biello, "Insects Provide Billions in Free Services," *Scientific American* (April 3, 2006), www.scientificamerican.com.

ACKNOWLEDGMENTS

Without the decision of two lovers decades ago, Foggy River Farm would never have come to fruition. So my first thank-you goes to Emmett's grandparents, John and Kay. They settled on these rolling hills and fertile floodplains and made the land their home. I wish I could have known them—although in some way, I think I do. Though gone now, they will both be here always.

A farm takes intergenerational commitment. The first to farm would have been the last were it not for those who followed: in this case, Bob and Toni. Thanks for offering wisdom and solace in turn, supporting our efforts with space and equipment, and tolerating our loudmouthed roosters, alpacas, sheep, goats, and dogs—not to mention our redneck porch constantly covered in feed sacks, buckets, lug bins, boots, and chicken turds. I'm starting to learn that grapes are pretty cool, too.

Emmett and I are not the only ones whose hands have touched Foggy River Farm: we appreciate the contributions of Enrique, Ismael, Susana and Austin, Sofie, poet Will, Angel and Socorro, and the Amys. And of course our hardworking hens, insane goats, beet-brained sheep, rodent-controlling cats, and dedicated farm dogs (including dear Kea who herds nothing but buzzards).

That covers the farm end of things, but a book takes an entirely different community. First thanks goes to my mom, who purchased countless books for her reading-obsessed daughter and always held firm in her belief that I could

Acknowledgments

become a doctor, sled-dog racer in Alaska, or even an author—whatever I set my mind to. Her support has carried me far, and I'm still working on her guesthouse. Mom, you're the best. I'm so glad you've brought Kevin and Marilyn into our lives; I couldn't ask for a better family.

I'd also like to thank Elizabeth Kaplan, without whom the book would have remained a distant dream. (Am I seriously a published author? Pinch me.) I am truly honored to have Elizabeth's dedication, follow-through, passion, and good humor on my side. She's one of those people who just gets things.

Thanks are due as well to Gary Luke, Rachelle Longé, and Erin Riggio, whom I got to know through phone, e-mail, and Word's Track Changes, respectively. (Erin: Sorry for the excess parentheticals. Also, at first I thought your initials were A.U.) I have come to appreciate that publishing a book takes a village, and I'm grateful to have had such inspired, independent villagers supporting mine. Thank you *all* for taking a chance on me, guiding me through the process, and crafting this into a story fit to move from an endless series of Word files to a real, honest-to-goodness, dead-tree book. I still can't believe it happened.

Teachers, like farmers, should be thanked more often. So I'd like to mention some of the teachers who taught me to write, and more important, to think: Julie Kennedy, Marvin Diogenes, Rick Barot and Malena Watrous, Ms. Zedalis, Mr. Goss, Mr. Up, and Dr. Hennessey. Deana Fabbro-Johnston, you are one of the most wonderful people in the world.

And of course, Emmett: my first reader, chief cheerleader, research assistant, rooster wrangler, love, and husband. It's fitting that this book begins and ends with you, and I hope that you think of the entire thing as a first chapter with many more to come.

ABOUT THE AUTHOR

Lynda Hopkins was born and raised in suburban San Diego, then moved north to study Earth Systems and Creative Writing at Stanford University. After graduating with a BS, BA, and MS, she traveled around New Zealand in a camper van with her boyfriend, working on homesteads, market farms, and a dairy. Late one night, the delusional duo decided to start a farm of their own.

Lynda published her first written work in third grade, and has written for local and regional newspapers and magazines since college. This is her first book. She currently lives and works on Foggy River Farm in Healdsburg, California, where she can be found fulfilling the duties of a produce farmer, milkmaid, livestock midwife, writer, and community journalist—which is to say, she's not sleeping much but is sleeping very soundly indeed.